FROM
FLAPPERS
TO
RAPPERS

FROM FLAPPERS TO RAPPERS

THE ORIGINS,
EVOLUTION, AND
DEMISE OF YOUTH
CULTURE

MARCEL DANESI

CANADIAN
SCHOLARS
Toronto | Vancouver

From Flappers to Rappers: The Origins, Evolution, and Demise of Youth Culture
Marcel Danesi

First published in 2018 by
Canadian Scholars, an imprint of CSP Books Inc.
425 Adelaide Street West, Suite 200
Toronto, Ontario
M5V 3C1

www.canadianscholars.ca

Library and Archives Canada Cataloguing in Publication

Danesi, Marcel, 1946-, author
    From flappers to rappers : the origins, evolution, and demise of youth culture / Marcel Danesi.

Includes bibliographical references and index.
Issued in print and electronic formats.
ISBN 978-1-55130-954-5 (softcover).--ISBN 978-1-55130-955-2 (PDF).--ISBN 978-1-55130-956-9 (EPUB)

    1. Youth--United States--History--20th century. 2. Popular culture--United States--History--20th century. 3. Subculture--United States--History--20th century. 4. United States--Social conditions--20th century. I. Title.

HQ796.D36 2018   305.235097309'04   C2018-900757-5
                                                   C2018-900758-3

Text design by Elisabeth Springate
Cover design by Em Dash Design

Printed and bound in Canada by Webcom

MIX
Paper from
responsible sources
FSC® C004071

CONTENTS

ACKNOWLEDGEMENTS

I would like to thank Debbie Smith-Shank of Ohio State University and Geoffrey Stewart of Western University for their truly insightful comments that made it possible for me to greatly improve this book. I also want to thank Stacy Costa for all her help in technical matters. I also wish to thank Natalie Garriga, my editor at CSP, for her support, insights, and overall enthusiasm. Finally, my gratitude really goes out to the many students who took my youth culture course. They are the real experts here. I could not have written this without them.

PREFACE

Youth is a dream, a form of chemical madness.

—F. Scott Fitzgerald (1896–1940)

In the mid-1950s, an unknown brash country-boy singer called Elvis Presley came onto the social radar after recording "Heartbreak Hotel," "Love Me Tender," "Hound Dog," and "Don't Be Cruel." It was obvious to one and all that something exciting was brewing. The music was fun, brash, electrifying, and different from anything that the staid society of the period was accustomed to hearing. That was the era when rock and roll turned every young person's life around—drastically. It was the ingredient that sparked what Fitzgerald called (in the epigraph above) the "chemical madness" of youth.

The excitement was infectious. It ensnared virtually everyone under the age of 20. Rock and roll had arrived to provide a new cultural environment for young people to come to grips with their hormonal chemistry; to affiliate with each other as a community, distinct from adults; and, more importantly, to start a social rebellion by proxy (through the music and its attendant lifestyle). The music stimulated in young people a desire to rebel against a boring, stale, and morally rigid adult culture, which also possessed prejudicial views of women and different races. Unconsciously, they felt that their unstated rebellion should make the world right. The hippie era was just around the corner; it brought the rebellion of the 1950s literally to the streets, radically changing the world. But the seeds of the rebellion go back considerably in time, well before Elvis Presley. Youth culture originated in the Roaring Twenties—a distinct, autonomous form of culture interrupted abruptly by the Great Depression and World War II. It was revived by the rock and roll rebels who followed Elvis and kept going right up to the millennium by subsequent generations of youths, from the hippies to the punks and the rappers. Many changes have resulted from youth movements over the course of the twentieth century. Racial discrimination, gender roles, and sexual repression, among other social issues, have been grappled with since the 1920s.

I have written this book to share with readers my interpretation of the importance of youth culture in North America and to discuss the likely reasons why it may be coming to an end. I have been inspired by the students in my undergraduate course on youth culture at the University of Toronto, a course that has been an absolute privilege to teach, or more exactly, to co-teach with the class members, since the real experts in the course are the students themselves. An earlier book of mine, *Geeks, Goths, and Gangstas*, was the first product of that class and the related research issues that it allowed me to pursue outside the classroom. This is a completely new book, shaped by the many events that have since induced me to change many of my previous views. I really want this book to be read by anyone and everyone who is interested in how and why, at least in my view, the modern world has become what it has become. It could be used both as an introductory text to the cultural study of youth and, at the same time, as a starting point for discussing the role of youth in the modern world.

I bear no hidden ideological agenda, or particular academic stance. I have written on youth and adolescence in previous works, in which I did at times take a stance. This book is different from those. I have lived through, and thus experienced firsthand, two youth movements—the early rock and roll one and the subsequent hippie one. I have also taught youths who have participated in the various subsequent youth movements, from punk to rap. I have thus approached the writing of this book from the perspective of both my personal experiences and the dialogue I have maintained with young people in my own classes throughout four decades of teaching at the university. I want to engage readers in the same dialogue, so that even if they disagree with everything I have written, I will consider having written it as worthwhile if it leads readers to at the very least contemplate the importance of youth in the constitution of the modern world.

I intend to delve into the *forma mentis* of youth and especially of the cultural systems and artifacts that young people created for themselves in the different eras. Adolescence and youth culture were always one and the same. This is no longer true. My conclusion will attempt to determine how we are evolving socially in an age where digital technologies may have brought about the demise of youth culture, as such, and what this implies for all of us.

CHAPTER 1

Origins: From the Construction of Adolescence to the Roaring Twenties

I looked back on the roaring Twenties, with its jazz, "Great Gatsby" and the pre-Code films as a party I had somehow managed to miss.

—*Hugh Hefner (1926–2017)*

PROLOGUE

On October 29 of 1923, a stage performance took place that signalled how radically American society, and, indeed, the modern Western world, was changing. The performance was a Broadway musical, called *Runnin' Wild*, that featured a sexually suggestive dance, called the Charleston, which became "wildly" popular (pun intended) among young people throughout America. It was, in retrospect, a veritable sign of the changing times, heralding the arrival of the so-called Roaring Twenties, an era that marked, perhaps for the first time in modern history, the emergence and spread of a new ("running wild") form of culture created, promoted, and performed (literally) by young people. The term *Twenties* in "Roaring Twenties" not only re-ferred to the decade of the 1920s but, suggestively, to the young people who were in their twenties in that decade and who led the way in promoting a new lifestyle that blatantly rejected the stodgy quasi-puritanical forms of adult society that constituted the cultural mainstream at the time.

It is not coincidental that an icon of early 1960s youth culture, Chubby Checker—best known for having made another dance, the Twist, a youth craze with his hit records—also recorded a song version of the Charleston in 1961, thus retrospectively linking young people in two significant decades of social change—the 1920s and the 1960s. In a phrase—if there is a starting point to the coalescence of a veritable "youth culture," separate from childhood and adulthood cultures, it is the Roaring Twenties. It was a distinctive era of sweeping social change, coming right after World War I and the worldwide epidemic known as the Spanish flu. It was spurred on by an abiding desire for a new freer lifestyle based on more liberal and lenient social mores, shedding the drudgery, condescension, and hypocrisy espoused by society's elders that had brought about the war and suffocating strictures on how young people were supposed to behave in the world.

The Roaring Twenties changed everything from fashion, Victorian gender models, and courtship rituals to views of morality and young people themselves as emotionally and socially different from the past and from society's elders. A "generation gap" (as it came to be called later) had crystallized that was symbolized by fads like the Charleston, jazz music, fashion trends such as flapper hats for females, and the like. It comes as no surprise to find that—in addition to Checker's rendition—there have been many subsequent recollections and reuses of this symbolic dance and song, perhaps indicating its momentous impact on the world. It is found, for example, in various films recalling the Roaring Twenties, such as *Roxie Hart* (1942), *Tea for Two* (1950), and *Midnight in Paris* (2011).

The post-war and post–Spanish flu young people wanted things to change, socially, politically, and morally. They pursued a carefree, open, non-traditional lifestyle, with its own music, fashions, and social rituals. Society's elders condemned what they saw as vulgar, crude, and symptomatic of moral decay. But they could not stem the tide, prodded by an openly sexual lifestyle and mood that was captured brilliantly by the 2002 movie *Chicago* (based on the 1975 Broadway musical).

This did not, however, deter society from trying to shut the social floodgates. The solution was Prohibition (as will be discussed). But all this did was entrench the new lifestyle even more, leading to a nightlife culture with its speakeasies (early night clubs) and dance halls catering to young people who went out at night to enjoy themselves, away from the watchful eyes of parents and authority figures, in open defiance to the whole Prohibition mindset. Prohibition was also incapable of stopping the ever-perceptive business world from taking advantage of the potentially lucrative new markets for the ever-expanding domain of youthful popular entertainments. The Roaring Twenties thus also established a synergy among the marketplace, art, and lifestyle patterns that continues to exist to this day. In America, when cultural change occurs, the marketplace seems to invariably jump on the bandwagon, often taking over its reins. For this reason, American popular culture has constantly come under criticism, ranging from the Frankfurt School scholars who saw the artistic movements produced by it as commodities similar to manufactured goods that could be easily discarded to those who saw it, and still see it, as a form of mind control by business and government.[1] Indeed, new businesses sprung up and older ones were transformed radically to cater to the ever-spreading "decadent" culture, as it came to be called. By the 1930s, the same type of culture had spread to all corners of the modern world. It could not be curtailed, despite the severity of the legislative measures taken by those in authority. The fledgling youth culture became more than a fun and entertaining experiment; it evolved into a driving force behind a seemingly constant need for change on the part of contemporary society.

This chapter will discuss and annotate the forces—social, political, technological, and cultural—that converged in the 1920s to bring about changes in the mindset of all people, which led to the establishment of both "adolescence" as a psychological category and "youth culture" as the locus where adolescents acted out their impulses and developed their own musical, literary, and artistic products. This new form of culture would not have spread broadly, however, if it had not dovetailed with the rise of the mass media, especially recordings, radio, and cinema, which started catering increasingly to the lifestyle preferences and predilections of young people. I will also discuss the views of F. Scott Fitzgerald and Ernest Hemingway, as well as the role played by art movements such as Dada and Futurism in shaping the ethos of the era.

ADOLESCENCE

For a distinct youth culture to emerge in the first place, a perception of post-pubescent individuals as emotionally, socially, and cognitively different from adults, was needed. That came from the relatively new science of psychology at the bridge between the nineteenth and twentieth centuries. Specifically, it was the publication of a pivotal book, *Adolescence*, by psychologist G. Stanley Hall in 1904, that established the post-pubescent period as psychologically differentiable.[2]

Hall defined adolescence as a regular stage of emotional, cognitive, and social development—a period of preparation for adulthood irrespective of culture or upbringing. He claimed that it was simply never acknowledged or recognized as such previously, and all that psychology did was identify it scientifically as a maturational stage. This went contrary to virtually all models of maturation of the past, which distinguished two main periods in the lifecycle—pre-puberty and post-puberty. And even in the twentieth century it took a while for the concept of adolescence to catch on and become a widespread accepted tenet of psychology and society. Indeed, in 1930, the Italian political theorist Antonio Gramsci made the following remark: "In the life of children there are two very clear-cut phases, before and after puberty."[3] Hall put all his theoretical eggs in the biology basket, ignoring that maybe adolescence was more of a social construct than a stage of maturation—a necessity of the times rather than a pattern rooted in biology. Certainly, before Hall, the passage from childhood to adulthood was seen as immediate at puberty. And even today, in some parts of the world, coming-of-age rites are still practised to signal the advent of maturation in a concrete way. There certainly was no concept of a transitional stage called adolescence before the late nineteenth century. This is evidenced by the fact that there were no special laws, social practices, theories, or institutions before that era related to adolescents. There were also no special views of childhood itself, such as those we have today. Children were seen, essentially, as "adults in the making." As late as 1708 in Britain, a child of seven could be hanged for stealing, and some of the most dangerous factory jobs in the subsequent Industrial Age were performed by children.

During the latter part of the Industrial Age, in cities throughout Europe, the view of childhood started changing because of the truly dire conditions into which children were projected. The industrialized workplace was an inhospitable one, and society began to take pity on children, who not only worked long hours but were increasingly taking to the streets for purposes of survival. The figure of the "street urchin" emerged in that era. In the factories and mechanical shops, children simply could not keep up with the pace or carry out the type of physically demanding labour required of them; nor could they handle the literacy requirements of the workplace. As a result, they were treated with harshness and barbarity—a brutal situation that has been imprinted indelibly into our collective memory by novels such as Charles Dickens' *Oliver Twist* (1838).

In a short time, specific laws were passed to protect children and, significantly, to keep them in school longer. It became illegal, for example, to send children out to work, or to hire them, until after puberty. At about the same time, Romantic writers started depicting childhood as a period of imagination, fantasy, innocence, and purity. Inspired by Jean-Jacques Rousseau's novel *Émile* (1762), novelists such as Robert Louis Stevenson (*Treasure Island*, 1883) and Rudyard Kipling (*The Jungle Book*, 1894) started carving a fantasy-land image of childhood into communal consciousness. It was an antidote, in retrospect, to the brutality of child labour. It intended to create, and did create, a new view of children as innocents, needing the entire prepubescent period to become mature not only physically but emotionally and socially. Not surprisingly, this image of childhood did not catch on broadly at first, and even today it does not exist in many parts of the world, where similar social, legal, and narrative traditions do not exist. Indeed, it is estimated that the number of what we in the West would define as "working children" is in the hundreds of millions worldwide. They are hardly perceived through the same rose coloured glasses with which we view childhood.

It was also towards the latter part of the nineteenth century that a scientific view of childhood as a psychologically crucial stage of development emerged. Influenced by social Darwinism, the practitioners of psychology (then in its infancy) claimed that children underwent adaptive stages of mental and emotional growth, as predictable as the stages of their bodily growth. Although controversial at first, it became such a widespread idea that, to this day, it is felt to be incontestable. Together, the new literature-based fantasy-land and scientific views of childhood had a profound impact on the fabric of urbanized society.

The redefinition of childhood was the catalyst for the creation of the new psychological category of adolescence, which had a specific social reason behind its construction—the need to keep post-pubescent individuals in school longer so that they could be better prepared for the new industrialized workplace and, simultaneously, to keep them off the streets, given an expanding crisis in job availability as the workplace was undergoing radical changes by the turn of the twentieth century. The term "adolescent" came into common usage already in the mid-1800s to refer to any person who stayed in school past puberty. The term was coined originally in the Middle Ages to refer to any male child who decided to move away from the family farm to work independently in some city guild or trade.[4] For five centuries subsequently, this meaning of the term remained virtually unchanged. Late in the eighteenth century, an important movement occurred in England called the "Sunday school movement," which was inaugurated to help poor, working children gain a basic level of literacy. By the time of large-scale urbanization, the movement expanded, as education for one and all became a practical necessity. Those who stayed in school beyond childhood were called adolescents. The original meaning of the word was lost once and for all.

As a growing number of the new breed of adolescents stayed in school for longer periods of time, they came to be perceived more and more as "older children," rather than young adults or quasi-adults, as they had been in every other previous era, for the simple reason that they remained economically dependent upon adults. By the early 1900s, people started to view adolescence increasingly as a phase of preparation for adulthood. This led, inevitably, to a host of unprecedented social problems among the adolescents themselves—unwanted pregnancies, an increase in the incidence of sexually transmitted diseases, alcoholism, street hooliganism, and so on and so forth. Clearly, nature could not be fooled by what was essentially a social construct. It was obvious to one and all that sexually mature individuals—post-pubescent individuals—could not be told *tout court* to ignore their sexual urges—to ignore their maturity—and concentrate on school as they did when they were children.

To make sure that the hormonal chemistry of pubescence did not get the better part of these "older children," complicated taboos emerged that got quickly incorporated into law. The new "restraining measures" brought about a growing sense that adolescents were inherently problematic, and that the adolescent period was "traumatic," as young people adjusted emotionally and sexually to their post-pubescent life. From these conditions, in 1904, as mentioned above, G. Stanley Hall put forth the claim that adolescence was a natural biological-psychological stage in human development marked by emotional turmoil because of the fact that the adolescent was adapting to conditions that were emotionally and socially different from those that characterized the world of childhood. Adolescence had become a self-fulfilling prophecy. To this day, we think of the post-pubescent period as constituting a transitional phase towards adulthood—a phase characterized by emotional problems that, in previous times, would undoubtedly have been viewed as bizarre. It is true, of course, that even the earliest civilizations differentiated between *young* and *old* as distinct stages of life. But the idea of adolescents as undergoing a maturational phase all its own emerged in full bloom at the start of the twentieth century.

The construction of adolescence as a psychological stage brought about a fundamental shift in Western groupthink. As psychologist Robert Epstein has aptly remarked,

> Through most of human history, young people were integrated into adult society early on, but beginning in the late 1800s, new laws and cultural practices began to isolate teens from adults, imposing on them an increasingly large set of restrictions and artificially extending childhood well past puberty.[5]

Epstein goes on to paint a pretty bleak picture of the consequences of this isolation. Suicide, for instance, has become a leading cause of death among teens, after accidents and homicides. Early in the twentieth century, in fact, scholars such as Émile Durkheim took the emergence of suicide outside of martyrdom as a symptom of modernity, right after adolescence became a reality.[6] So, Epstein asks, is our socially constructed view of the coming-of-age period really necessary? As pointed out elsewhere,[7] there is much more to the whole question of adolescence than seeing it as a consequence of modernity. There may, in actual fact, have always been what we call adolescents in the past, but they were either marginalized, repressed, or at the very least ignored and expected to assume adult responsibilities at puberty. For such reasons, young people were rarely given a chance to express themselves independently, unless they belonged to an elite class, such as the nobility. We may indeed have constructed adolescence artificially, but the construction may have been a blessing in disguise, as will be argued in this book. There probably would not have been a Roaring Twenties or a counterculture movement in the 1960s—both socially liberating and enfranchising movements—without the construction of adolescence as a distinct period of growth.

Adolescence as a reality became entrenched, psychologically and socially, by compulsory high school education. High schools have always provided the social conditions in which adolescent behaviours materialize and run their course. The high school is an adolescence-preserving locus; it is where adolescents form groups, allegiances, worldviews, and romantic entanglements. Of course, not all adolescents participate in the social universe of the high school—often at high emotional risk. As youth researcher Penelope Eckert observes, although the majority of teens "center their lives around the school and its activities," there are "those who reject the hegemony of the school" altogether.[8] And there are runaways and street kids who often populate the downtown cores of major urban areas. These kids develop a "streetwise" form of adolescence. Also, within the school there are always outliers, who see their time at school exclusively as preparation for the real world and for the cultivation of knowledge. For most, though, high school has been (at least until today) where friendships are forged, clique allegiances established, conflictual behaviours developed, social personae within the school manufactured, and so on. The school is an enclave for both taming the youthful hormones, so to speak, and allowing them to coalesce chemically. Newcomers are required, typically, to pass implicit initiation rites or to suffer ridicule at first; outsiders are looked upon with suspicion and must be introduced into the enclave by a school member, or else they are marginalized.

The emotional power of the high school was portrayed brilliantly by the late controversial writer J.D. Salinger in his compelling novel *The Catcher in the Rye*, published in book form in 1951—a book to which we will return. Suffice it to say at this point that Salinger provided an unforgettable portrait of what adolescence had become by the late 1940s. It was at this point in North American social history that the term *teenager* gained general currency within the mainstream culture, providing verbal evidence that a new social persona had indeed come into being. The term goes back to the late 1930s, when the Fair Labor Standards Act in the United States set the minimum age of 14 for employment outside school hours. Also, in 1944, *Seventeen*, a magazine for teenagers themselves, no less, began publication. Young people had emerged as a social and economic force to be reckoned with.

ROMANTICISM

Adolescence is as much a social construction as it is a Romantic notion. By the late 1800s, Romanticism had emerged as a powerful mindset throughout Europe, emphasizing ideals, inspiration, subjectivity, and the primacy of the individual. The figure of the adolescent fit perfectly into this mindset. Romanticism and the expanding Industrialist world had become unwitting partners in promoting the concept of adolescence broadly. The period of adolescence was portrayed as an emotionally traumatic and rebellious one by writers such as Wolfgang von Goethe already at the end of the eighteenth century. His novel *The Sorrows of Young Werther* (1774) depicted the idealism and angst of youth. The novel became so popular that it even caused young men to dress imitatively like the protagonist in the novel.

By the start of the twentieth century, young people were seen as different from adults. This gradually changed everything. Marriage, for example, was delayed considerably compared to the past. The average age for marriage up to the late nineteenth century was a few years after puberty. By the mid-1950s, it was 20. Today, it is being postponed even more, on average, and viewed as an option not a necessity. Today's young people are expected to delay adult responsibilities and marriage until much later than at any other time in human history.

Hall's theory of adolescence was also fundamentally Romantic. He claimed that the main phases in the life cycle—childhood, adolescence, adulthood—constituted a kind of "recapitulation" of the stages that characterized the evolution of the human race—a quintessentially Romantic idea that can be traced to writers such as Rousseau. Accordingly, the infant recapitulated humanity's animal stage, the adolescent the savage one, and the adult the mature (sapient) stage. Predictably, Hall went on, the passage from one stage to the other was a difficult one, for the reason that transitions require adaptation and adjustment. Undoubtedly, Hall's theory would have been quickly discarded as fanciful speculation if not for the fact that the Industrialist society of the era needed it as a rationalization (if not justification) for having called into existence the "problems of adolescence" through social construction. Coming at the end of the Romantic period, Hall's proposal put the finishing touches on the portrait of adolescence that was crystallizing throughout society. Goethe's Young Werther had migrated from fiction into the real world.

Following on Hall's coattails, Sigmund Freud claimed that adolescence was experienced as traumatic because of repressive childhood experiences.[9] Freud's proposal, which initially met with criticism, made its way into the mainstream of psychology. Although later psychologists attenuated it somewhat, by pointing out that cultural factors other than childhood sexual repressions played a role in adolescence, it nevertheless became an unconscious pattern in the modern mindset. Freud's "trauma theory" goes somewhat like this: Inhabiting a strange new sexual body, adolescents start to feel awkward, anxious, and guilty (or afraid) about their repressed desires and feelings. Consequently, they are besieged by a pervasive awareness of, and sensitivity to, what others think of them. Membership in a peer group is their way of gaining shelter from the ravaging effects of the coming-of-age stage. The peer group serves, therefore, as an enclave sheltering adolescents from the emotional burdens of puberty and allowing their repressions to be channelled through in-group social interaction. But Freud's theory was no more than a clinical interpretation of the *Sturm und Drang* (German for "storm and stress") literary movement which started with the 1776 Romantic play of the same name by Friedrich Maximilian von Klinger in which youthful passionate subjectivity is highlighted. And, as just mentioned, the image of a highly sensitive young individual struggling against conventional society came originally from Goethe's *The Sorrows of Young Werther*. Arguably, psychology itself can be seen to be a product of Romanticism, with its emphasis on the individual as possessing unique emotions at various ages.

The psychologist who came most under the influence of Freud, becoming one of the most acclaimed theorists of adolescence since mid-twentieth century, is Erik Erikson, who was instrumental in developing the modern concept of *identity*— the awareness one has of oneself as a whole person.[10] Erikson modified Freud's ideas somewhat, seeing upbringing and cultural influences as significant to the formation of the adolescent. He characterized the adolescent period as a stage of "identity crisis." Such a crisis may occur when an adolescent struggles with inner conflicts before gaining a sense of purpose and moving into adulthood, having passed through developmental phases that lead to a sense of self-worth or, as he called it, "ego identity." Although it is largely a natural biological stage of development, Erikson suggested that the experience of adolescence is given its particular shape by the culture in which the individual is reared. Accordingly, adolescents are purported to search for an identity through "role diffusion," that is, through some form of identification with a "hero" or a "leader" to the extent of paradoxically even losing their own developing identities, surrendering them to the leader.

Again, all this makes sense if we understand that the "psychology of adolescence" is a derivative of the Romantic view of young people as idealists who seek to understand themselves apart from adult society. It set the stage for the emergence of a "youth culture" and the expectation that young people would engage in lifestyles that were different from the adult ones. This expectation became an ingrained social principle by the 1920s in America. While many saw the new lifestyle choices of young people as inevitable responses to the Sturm und Drang of adolescence, the young people themselves simply came to expect and enjoy the new social freedoms that were emerging. But this principle was challenged by some as being culture-specific, rather than a fact of life across the world. Already in the 1920s, anthropologist Margaret Mead had assembled a large amount of data on Samoan society that told a different story. She warned that the emotional traumas that American adolescents were purported to undergo were not reflexes of a natural adaptive stage in the human life cycle but rather offshoots of the social construction of adolescence.[11] Mead reported that Samoan pubescent individuals experienced no drastic change in personality as they passed from childhood to adulthood and the advent of puberty was not felt, in any way whatsoever, to be traumatic. This was because Samoan children were expected to take on the responsibilities of adulthood the instant they reached puberty. Simply put, Mead found that the traditional Samoan culture had young adults, but it did not have adolescents. Culture, she maintained, had created the conditions that fostered "adolescent traumas," not nature.

The gist of her research implied that adolescence as a stressful and traumatic period of growth, characterized by a need to reject existing social mores with open contumacious displays of rebellion against any and every authority figure, was culture-specific. As Mead described it, the growth of female Samoan adolescents, for instance, was continuous and smooth, not interrupted and jagged. The young Samoan girl assumed her new role in the world by participating in adult activities—caring for children, catching fish, cleaning house, and engaging in dances and rituals. Pubescent boys and girls partook freely in courtship without any sense of guilt or shame. Mead painted the following portrait of Samoan adolescence:

> Adolescence represented no period of crisis or stress but was instead an orderly developing of a set of slowly maturing interests and activities. The girls' minds were perplexed by no conflicts, troubled by no philosophical queries, beset by no remote ambitions. To live as a girl with many lovers as long as possible, and then marry in one's own village, near one's own relatives, and to have many children, these were uniform and satisfying ambitions.[12]

In Samoa, there was no preoccupation with body image, no anxiety over sexual identity. As a consequence, a separate youth-based lifestyle did not emerge in the Samoan culture of the era. As an aside, the fact that Samoa now also has adolescent lifestyles in the Western sense of the word is testament to the fact that in the global village attitudes, trends, and worldviews move freely about influencing each other, although most of the influence tends to come from modern societies such as America. In the same period that Mead was studying Samoan youth, America had engendered the first true distinct youth culture—with its own patterns of fashion, music, symbolism, language, lifestyle, rituals, and so on. In high schools across America, adolescents started to see them-selves more and more as socially different from adults. And this perception spilled over into society at large, which was starting to see youthful lifestyles and mores as inevitable, at least during the period of adolescence and early adulthood.

FLAPPERS

The high school became a "community" in the sociological sense of the word by the 1910s—that is, it was increasingly evolving into a self-contained social system within the larger society. By the 1920s, researchers Robert and Helen Lynd made the following relevant statement: "The high school, with its athletics, clubs, sororities and fraternities, dances and parties, and other extracurricular activities is a fairly complete social cosmos in itself, and about this city within a city the social life of the intermediate generation centers."[13] The daily life of a young person was becoming evermore anchored within this "social cosmos," as the Lynds characterized it. Adolescents started to see the high school as the central locus for gaining and maintaining social status within their own peer community, primarily through symbolic codes (language, dress), actions (going to parties, engaging primarily with peers), and behaviours (engagement in musical trends) that were deemed by the community to be socially advantageous. Young people sought, like never before, to gain overall acceptance, status, and prestige within the high school through a skillful manipulation of what soon came to be called "coolness." This sense of independence from adult society extended to the after-school period, when young people in their 20s entered the workforce but at the same time sought to maintain a fun-filled lifestyle that was markedly different from the Victorian-based puritanical lifestyle of adult America at the time.

As mentioned, Prohibition came forward as an attempt to thwart the ever-spreading youth movement, an attempt (at least in part) to stem the rise of a freer lifestyle based on sexual openness and booze. As it turned out, it had the opposite effect, leading to bootlegging and the rise of a nightlife that promoted drinking, dancing, smoking, and partying in locales called, euphemistically, speakeasies. There never was a comparable locale in America until Prohibition unwittingly brought it into being. It seems that if you prohibit something, then it becomes more attractive and alluring by going underground.

Prohibition started in the first decades of the twentieth century. But it really took a foothold in 1920, when a prohibition amendment—the 18th Amendment—was added to the US Constitution. Many people ignored the national ban and drank illegal beverages supplied by networks of bootleggers. The amendment was eventually abolished in 1933. Those who were responsible for Prohibition believed, fervently, that alcohol damaged health and, more importantly, corrupted moral behaviour, as well as fostered poverty. But there were hidden motives at play here. One of these was xenophobia. Some people felt that the large numbers of recent immigrants to America would become more "American" if their drinking habits were changed. Another was religious zealotry. Many religious denominations taught that drinking alcohol was immoral. Between 1880 and World War I in 1914, many states adopted prohibition or local-option laws. In 1913, Congress passed the Webb-Kenyon Act, which forbade the mailing or shipping of liquor into any state that banned alcohol. When the United States entered World War I in 1917, most Americans considered prohibition an appropriate patriotic sacrifice. In December 1917, the US Congress approved the 18th Amendment to the Constitution.

But a hidden motive for Prohibition that is rarely pointed out is sexism—the fear that young women would imbibe alcohol and become sexually promiscuous. The strategy failed, since it actually sped up the liberation of women, leading to a freer lifestyle for young women who came to be known more generally as "flappers." The flappers were intent on enjoying themselves openly by flouting the sexist restrictive standards of behaviour for women at the time. The flapper movement is the true beginning of women's liberation in the sense that it allowed women to be as sexual in public as they wanted. The flappers were distinguished by the hats they wore and their short dresses and stylish shoes, adorned with fringe, beads, and spangles. They sported short "bobbed" hair—a very subversive trend for women in that era. If there is one image that can be pinpointed as symbolizing the start of youth culture, it probably is that of the defiant flapper.

Photo 1.1: Silent Film Actress Norma Talmadge in a Flapper Style

Source: Library of Congress, Prints & Photographs Division, LC-DIG-ggbain-35550

Flappers were part of a broader youth movement; they were joined by their male counterparts, known as "flaming youth," describing the free lifestyle they led outside of school and work and the flamboyant clothing they wore. Together they partied and met up at the speakeasies late at night. At these locales, they drank bootleg liquor, listened to jazz, and engaged in sexually suggestive behaviour. Hollywood saw the lucrative side of the flapper movement, producing popular movies such as *The Idle Class* (1921), *Speedy* (1928), *Piccadilly* (1929), and *Pandora's Box* (1929). Hollywood also became a social commentator, as can be seen in the 1939 movie *The Roaring Twenties*, which is a retrospective on an era characterized by crisis and change. The 2002 movie *Chicago* has more recently encapsulated the ethos of the era by portraying the sense of liberation and fun that women experienced, perhaps for the first time in modern history, and at the same time the dangerous and hypocritical stances towards women that the era represented.

Society's elders and moral guardians condemned the flappers, seeing their lifestyle as a momentary aberration in the evolution of American womanhood. It was not. The flapper attitude entered the cultural mainstream in 1923—the year in which, as mentioned at the beginning of this chapter, *Runnin' Wild* helped transform the Charleston, a dance loved by the flappers, into a craze for the young (and the young at heart) throughout the nation. The American psyche was secretly yearning for a new carefree and permissive lifestyle. By the early 1930s, this desire was spreading to all corners of American society and to other parts of the world as well. Its emotional power could not be curtailed, despite the severity of the legislative measures taken, from Prohibition to various forms of censorship (direct or indirect). Its profane spirit was then, and is now, an unstoppable social force, challenging stodgy moralism and aesthetic pretentiousness in tandem. Ever since the flappers, youth culture has been a driving force behind American social change, triggering an unprecedented society-wide debate about art, sex, and "true culture" that is still relevant. There would have been no counterculture movement without the flappers; nor would there would have been, at about the same time, a women's lib movement.

The Roaring Twenties really did change American values and attitudes radically. Gender and race equality movements trace their origins indirectly to the flappers. By simply acting in a way that was fundamentally subversive to the status quo, they showed everyone that there were other ways to live and interact with each other, including African Americans especially through the marvellous musical art that they were creating at the time, known as jazz. The embracing of jazz by white youths brought about a subtle yet veritable revolution—the view that blacks are artists and not just former slaves. Jazz caught on like wildfire, bringing out the fact that young people were involved in a form of culture of their own making—a culture that was slowly spreading to the mainstream, blending in seamlessly with it. Jazz and sexually suggestive dancing became the norm. A social evolutionary process had started in earnest, thanks to the Roaring Twenties. Young people had made a special niche for themselves in American society, and the process of change that they initiated could not be reversed or stopped.

As feminist researcher Linda Scott has perceptively observed, the flappers were silent revolutionaries, bringing about changes in social attitudes by dressing provocatively, smoking cigarettes (and cigars), drinking booze, driving automobiles, and dancing frenetically in public.[14] The flappers "scared the heck," colloquially speaking, out of society's puritanical and prejudicial moral guardians. Scott puts it concisely as follows: "This era [the Roaring Twenties] brought a wave of sensualism, in which legions of young women—particularly though not exclusively those of modest means—asserted themselves by their dress, their dancing, and their romances."[15]

Photo 1.2: Betty Boop

Source: Image by Max Fleischer, courtesy of Wikimedia Commons

The flapper lifestyle was a target of satire early on. The best known one was the cartoon figure of Betty Boop, who appeared in the *Talkartoon* and *Betty Boop* film series, released by Paramount Pictures. Betty Boop satirized flapperism at the same time that she challenged the vacuous morals of the era with her childish and large round baby face, big eyes, and button nose. Betty Boop wore a coiffure; she had a small body and little bust. She always assumed a suggestive posture, complete with short skirt and high heel shoes. The censors of the 1930s required her image to be toned down and appear more demure. Betty Boop remains, to this day, one of the most recognizable cartoon characters of all time.

The movie retrospective on the speakeasy culture that came after the Flapper Era was *Casablanca*, directed by Michael Curtiz. The film is a romantic melodrama starring Humphrey Bogart and Ingrid Bergman. It was first shown publicly in 1942 and officially released in 1943. The narrative is set in the Moroccan city of Casablanca during the early years of World War II. The main characters are a cynical American adventurer named Rick Blaine (Bogart) and a lovely and luscious European woman named Ilsa Lund (Bergman), his sweetheart. Rick operates the popular nightclub "Rick's Café" in the city, which is under Nazi occupation. The movie's theme song, "As Time Goes By," is, at one level, a veiled nostalgic paean to the Roaring Twenties and, at another, an acknowledgement that things change. Ilsa asks the piano player to "Play it, Sam," a famous line often misquoted as "Play it again, Sam," acknowledging the nostalgic subtext of the movie.

The symbolic props used in *Casablanca* encapsulated the ethos of the early nightlife. Cigarettes, for example, are everywhere. Swaggering imperiously in his realm, Rick is rarely seen without a cigarette in his mouth or in his hand. So captivating was this image of nightclub "cool" to young cinemagoers that it became a lifestyle paradigm imitated by hordes of people in the subsequent 1950s—a paradigm satirized by Jean-Luc Godard in his 1960 film *Breathless*. In one scene, the main protagonist, Jean-Paul Belmondo, stares at a poster of Bogart in a cinema window. He takes out a cigarette and starts smoking it, imitating Bogart in *Casablanca*. With the cigarette dangling from the side of his mouth, Belmondo approaches his female mate with a blunt "Sleep with me tonight?" In Nicholas Ray's 1955 movie *Rebel without a Cause*, the sexual cool associated with smoking comes out forcefully in the "car chicken" scene, in which James Dean can be seen dangling a cigarette from the side of his mouth, just before he gets ready to duel his opponent to death with his car.

Casablanca is set during World War II. It was the war, in fact, that temporarily blocked the evolution of youth culture. Wars need young people to fight, not to dance and sing the night away. But the movement was reinvigorated right after the war in the 1950s by the boomer generation, as will be discussed in the next chapter.

THE JAZZ ERA

There is no youth culture without music to give it emotional substance. All other aspects of the culture are derivatives of the music or else intertwined with it. The Roaring Twenties era was also designated the Jazz Era, acknowledging that a new musical idiom had come forth to define it socially and aesthetically. Jazz was the fuel that propelled the first era of youth culture. It was the music of choice of the flappers, the flaming youth, and their milieu. It was new and exciting and broke radically from tradition. In its syncopations and blues-based melodies and harmonies it was iconoclastic. And, in a racially problematic environment, it came out of the souls of black Americans. Indeed, it was America's first homegrown music and masterful art form. Elders condemned it; the flappers, along with writers and artists, embraced it unabashedly.

One could say that jazz made music itself popular in a new way—as part of an unconscious aesthetic that spoke to young people in particular. But jazz did not emerge as popular in a historical vacuum. America's secret penchant for the profane can be traced back to vaudeville and musical comedy, which emerged during the late 1800s preparing the way for the Jazz Era to foment. Vaudeville consisted of singers, dancers, comedians, and other acts on the same program. But the performers were mainly all white, as were the audiences. At about the same time, music publishing centred in an area in New York City known as Tin Pan Alley entered the scene to spread music as a popular art, appealing to many except, perhaps, young people who were starting to find the music too tame and bland. But Tin Pan Alley also produced musical comedy, which, in some ways prefigured the lifestyle revolution that was just around the corner. One of the Tin Pan Alley composers, George Gershwin, would eventually come to embrace the jazz idiom and incorporate it brilliantly into a collage of classical, Tin Pan, and jazz styles that produced some of the greatest musical works of America, including his opera *Porgy and Bess* (1934).

After the Civil War, ironically it was the South that became a locus for the emergence of black music that started flourishing even among whites who (perhaps secretly) relished its vigour and rhythmic power, including the heart-wrenching songs called the blues and the exciting choral music associated with Southern black religion and its gospel basis—hence the term "gospel music." Night bars became the setting for the music, as portrayed in *Casablanca*. The piano replaced other instruments, leading to the jazz piano ensemble. Ragtime, a predecessor of jazz, was played almost exclusively on the piano. It became popular throughout America and flourished at the turn of the twentieth century, laying the groundwork for the Jazz Era. As a distinct style, jazz made its appearance in New Orleans around 1900. Rooted in dance music, it soon blended with the blues. The music was powerful and provocative, socially and aesthetically.

But jazz culture would have disappeared from the social radar screen if it were not for technology. Without the new mass media to spread jazz through radio and recordings, it would have remained localized, mainly in the South. The synergy between technology and youth culture was, in fact, established in the Jazz Era; without it there would be no youth culture as we know it today.

Sound recordings emerged in 1877, becoming an important channel for distributing popular music in the early 1900s—indeed for making it "popular." Soon after, records surpassed sheet music as the primary medium through which music was promoted and

Photo 1.3: Louis Armstrong

Source: Library of Congress, Prints & Photographs Division, NYWT&S Collection, LC-USZ62-127236

sold. Musical trends were now in the hands of performers and record companies, with the latter exploiting new markets. The first recordings of jazz were made in 1917 by a group of white musicians called the Original Dixieland Jass Band, followed by the first blues recordings in 1920. Both genres were eventually recorded by black musicians such as Louis Armstrong, Bessie Smith, and Ma Rainey. As jazz hit the radio airwaves, it un- furled pent-up emotions that were about to come out in a society where young people were expected to be obedient, go to school, go to work, get married, and settle down. Radio also allowed for new styles and genres of jazz to emerge and spread. One of the most popular was "swing," which led to the Big Band Era in the subsequent 1930s and 1940s, headed by band leaders, black and white, such as Count Basie, Duke Ellington, Benny Goodman, and Glenn Miller, thus showing that youth culture was largely colour blind when it came to music.

One of the key elements of jazz is improvisation or the ability to create musical ideas spontaneously within a harmonic and melodic frame. Improvisation had great appeal, since it implicitly broke down pre-established structures. This likely tapped into an unconscious impulse in young people to break down barriers, moral and social, and to lead the way in social change in an analogously improvised fashion. In other words, jazz epitomized the budding youth movement, unconsciously simulating its emotional rhythms. During its history, jazz has absorbed influences from folk and classical music, evolving into a magnificent musical art form. But it did not start out that way. It was a voice of change—a breaking away from boredom and stodginess.

With its broadcasts of live performances by a growing number of jazz musicians, radio led to an increasing demand for the music. One of the first heroes of youth culture was in fact a jazz musician—Louis Armstrong. This was truly remarkable, given the discrimination against blacks in that era. Armstrong made some of his most famous recordings with his own Hot Five and Hot Seven combos. These rank among the early masterpieces of jazz, along with his duo recordings is the same period with pianist Earl "Fatha" Hines. Armstrong also popularized scat singing—that is, wordless syllables sung to a beat.

The Jazz Era gave way to the Swing Era, which set a pattern for the evolution of youth culture in subsequent generations—whereby a trend would start among young people and gradually get adopted and normalized by the mainstream culture. The first hero of the Swing Era was Benny Goodman, a white musician who became known as the "King of Swing." Starting in 1934, Goodman's bands and combos brought swing to nationwide audiences through ballroom performances, recordings, and radio broadcasts. He was the first bandleader to feature black and white musicians playing together in public—an incredible event for the times. From swing, another major musical trend emerged, which constituted the boundary line between the early youth culture based on jazz and its second phase in the 1950s based on rock and roll, as will be discussed in the next chapter. That style that crossed the line was called "boogie-woogie." The music had an intense rhythm that created excitement through the repetition of a single phrase and a moving bass line that gave it an edge that was very appealing.

Jazz vocalists actually came into prominence as the first true "pop stars" during the swing and boogie-woogie eras, many singing with big bands. These included iconic stars such as Ella Fitzgerald, Billie Holiday, Nat King Cole, Carmen McRae, and Sarah Vaughan. All of them were young when they started out—significantly showing that jazz, like the performers, had come of age, appealing to young and old. Actually, because of World War II, which put a temporary halt to the "fun," a new kind of social consciousness had surfaced, uniting everyone regardless of age, gender, or race.

THE MASS MEDIA

As mentioned, without the mass media youth culture would never have fomented and evolved. The rise of jazz as a mass art and its successor, swing, was made possible by recordings and radio broadcasting, which made the music available to large audiences, converting it from a form of local expression to a commodity for one and all. The film screen also contributed greatly to the spread of youthful lifestyles. Its first stars were young people who acted and dressed and behaved like the flappers and the flaming youth, including Greta Garbo and Rudolph Valentino.

The synergy among technology, the mass media, and youth is a constant and ongoing one—and as will be argued in the final chapter it is also, paradoxically, the factor that may be bringing about a demise of youth culture. Youth culture has been largely a technologically constructed culture, reinforced by culture industries that influence our perception of young people and their trends; making us participants in its products and processes whether or not we are conscious of the factors at play. The social fabric of American culture in the Roaring Twenties was molded by youthful trends; in the 1950s, it was shaped by new mass media technologies, especially television, that spread the emerging rock and roll culture broadly; in the 1960s, it was shaped by hippie culture, which garnered media attention through protest and radical ideological proposals, changing society drastically; in the 1970s, it revolved around punk and disco; in the 1980s, it was shaped by an admixture, with experiments in sexual personae as emblemized by pop stars such as Madonna and Michael Jackson; in the 1990s, it was influenced by rap and hip-hop and promoted by music television. Even more telling is the fact many of the different musicians of each era, such as the Rolling Stones and Bob Dylan, have become cultural icons. The Rolling Stones' music is no longer limited to the baby boomer generation—young and old can partake in the music by simply clicking on a YouTube video. Suffice it to say that, at this point, cyberspace has had a profound impact on reconfiguring previous notions and constructions, such as the generation gap, that had relevance and resonance in previous eras.

As Marshall McLuhan emphatically argued, improvements in media technologies provide the means for both showcasing and inventing social trends.[16] The rise of American big business and advertising, based on technological possibilities and changes, has in fact resulted in a social system that has defined itself, until recently, through youth trends, whereby the views of older adults on everything from politics to music are labelled as "old fashioned" and "out of date." What emerged in the 1920s was, in fact, a social revolution, an ideological *coup d'état* that brought about the view that the path towards maturation and adulthood necessarily passed through adolescence. By the late 1920s, the cheapness and availability of mass-produced records and the ubiquity of radio led to a true shift in cultural aesthetics—the entrenchment of youth-based music as mainstream music. As mentioned, the war changed things for a while. Glenn Miller disbanded his highly popular band in 1942 and enlisted in the US Army, where he formed the 42-piece all-star Army Air Force Band, which entertained World War II service personnel with regular radio broadcasts. In 1944, Miller died when his small plane, headed to Paris, disappeared over the English Channel during bad weather. His influence was unmistakable. In the years subsequent to the war, Miller-style swing music developed into a society-wide craze.

Another critical aspect contributing to the establishment of youth culture is advertising, which started to flourish in the 1920s. The modern history of brands and youth culture overlap considerably.[17] It was in the Roaring Twenties, in fact, that advertising evolved into a science of persuasion intended to influence people to perceive objects of consumption as necessary accoutrements of life, leading to a widespread insatiable appetite for new things. With the entrenchment of electronic media (radio and television) in the 1940s and 1950s as mass communication outlets, advertising became itself a mass communication strategy, imprinting into groupthink the perception that objects of consumption were necessarily intertwined with the style and content of everyday life—a perception reinforced today through Internet advertising. As James B. Twitchell aptly puts it, "language about products and services has pretty much replaced language about all other subjects."[18] There is little doubt that the mass marketing and branding of products that started in the 1920s became part of the chemistry of youth culture. To this day, brands advertise primarily to young people, since they are the buyers of items that are significant to their milieu. Today it is mobile devices; in the 1920s it was hats and shoes. The Frankfurt School philosopher Herbert Marcuse articulated this relationship eloquently as follows:

> If mass communications blend together harmoniously, and often unnoticeably, art, politics, religion, and philosophy with commercials, they bring these realms of culture to their common denominator—the commodity form. The music of the soul is also the music of salesmanship. Exchange value, not truth value, counts.[19]

FITZGERALD, HEMINGWAY, DADA, AND FUTURISM

To really grasp what defines an age and its social ethos, one must turn to the writers and artists of the era. They can stand outside the cultural flow and observe its characteristics and implications better than anyone else. The flapper lifestyle was captured by cinema and by cartoonists, including Max Fleisher, creator of Betty Boop, and John Held, Jr., whose delightful pictures of the manners and pastimes of the Roaring Twenties conveyed the character of the era in humorous fashion. Held's cartoons were elegant and sophisticated, like the fashionable, fun-loving flappers he portrayed.

Two writers of the era merit special attention for providing an insightful and discerning narrative portrait of the Roaring Twenties—F. Scott Fitzgerald and Ernest Hemingway. The former was undoubtedly the leading writer of the era, and one of its glittering heroes, alongside jazz musicians and cinema stars.

Fitzgerald was both a participant in the high and decadent life he wrote about and a detached observer of its exciting rhythms, ideologies, and overall ethos. His early readers saw only the light side of Fitzgerald, as the critical reviews showed, putting him into the same realm as pulp fiction writers and thus leaving him generally unrecognized as a gifted writer. Most readers considered his stories a chronicle and even a celebration of moral decline. Only later have we come to realize that Fitzgerald's works were penetrating narrative portraits of what was happening to the American psyche as it moved away from its Victorian mindset to a lifestyle revolutionized by new technologies, including the automobile and the radio, which allowed America to liberate itself from its morally prosaic past and to enter the modern world, and even make it what it has become.

His first novel, *This Side of Paradise* (1920), anticipated the pleasure-seeking generation of the Jazz Era. He followed it up with *The Beautiful and Damned* (1922), and two collections of short stories, *Flappers and Philosophers* (1920) and *Tales of the Jazz Age* (1922). As the titles themselves reveal, Fitzgerald not only understood what was going on but may have been the one to name the events and the social figures himself. But it was his masterpiece, *The Great Gatsby* (1925), that truly unravelled the soul of the era. The novel centres around Jay Gatsby, a wealthy bootlegger, through whom Fitzgerald offers up a biting criticism of the moral emptiness of the affluent society of the era and its many contrasts—it was decadent, yet exciting; it was immoral, yet still in the grasp of moralism; and above all else, it was youthful, yet also mature. As Ernest Hemingway later remarked, it was something that could only be understood by those who were decadent: "Decadence is a difficult word to use since it has become little more than a term of abuse applied by critics to anything they do not yet understand or which seems to differ from their moral concepts."[20] In Fitzgerald's *Tender Is the Night* (1934), we get a glimpse into the origins of party and nightlife culture. Indeed, the whole concept of the party is an invention of the Jazz Era, spurred on by Prohibition, as was the indulgence of youth. As he so insightfully put it: "Grown up, and that is a terribly hard thing to do. It is much easier to skip it and go from one childhood to another."[21] Fitzgerald's characters are flappers and flaming youth, attempting to discover life not through sacrifice but through pleasure.

Fitzgerald's desire for extravagant living and a need for lots of money to sustain it led to personal disaster. It is little wonder that he became an alcoholic, especially after the mental breakdown of his wife, Zelda. Ironically, a few years after his death, his books won him the recognition he had desired while alive and would have provided him with the financial resources to live the life of Jay Gatsby.

Ernest Hemingway was also a product of the Jazz Era; like Fitzgerald, he was both a participant and a detached observer. He created a male character, sometimes called the "Hemingway Hero," who faces violence and destruction with courage, possessing what he called "grace under pressure"—that is, unemotional behaviour even in dangerous situations. In 1921, Hemingway went to Paris, where he met a number of young and disillusioned American writers for whom he became the principal spokesperson. The writers are sometimes called the "Lost Generation." Hemingway's most famous novels are *The Sun Also Rises* (1926) and *A Farewell to Arms* (1929). The former portrays a group of Americans who, like the Lost Generation, were disillusioned by the war; the latter, set in Italy during World War I, is a tragic love story.

Hemingway's stint in Paris no doubt injected a bohemian tinge into his portrait of 1920s America—a tinge that he acquired from interactions with the members of the Lost Generation. That name was used, and continues to be used, as a moniker for the entire Jazz Era. The principal figures in the group, in addition to Hemingway and Fitzgerald, were Gertrude Stein, Ezra Pound, E.E. Cummings, John Dos Passos, Thornton Wilder, and Hart Crane. They helped establish many of the stylistic and thematic foundations of modern literature and its emphasis on youth and existential angst. Stein was the one who reportedly coined the term "Lost Generation," a phrase Hemingway used in the preface to his novel *The Sun Also Rises*—"You are all a lost generation." The novel describes the loss of traditional faith, values, and personal direction among a group of Americans living in Europe.

The writings of Fitzgerald and Hemingway provide a language for discussing the philosophical changes that were occurring in society in the 1920s. Even single words can provide snapshots of a cultural era, as journalist John Morrish remarks.[22] For example, the word *cool*, which has been used by generation after generation of young people, emerged actually in the fifteenth century as a term of approval, suggesting calm and refrain. But its modern revival is traced to the Jazz Era. In the 1920s, jazz was hot, fast, and passionate; by the late 1940s, a softer more romantic jazz style was catching on, tracing its inspiration to Charlie Parker's 1947 *Cool Blues*. The title appealed instantly, and the word *cool* spread in the 1950s among teens to indicate an attractive person. You were either cool or you were not. In effect, the term allowed teens to make up their own minds as to the social qualities of their peers. *Cool* was recycled in the 1960s and 1970s by the hippies to indicate a new philosophical stoicism and behavioural nonchalance with respect to mainstream culture, extending its meaning considerably to fit in with the new hippie view of the world.[23] But philosophical "cool" starts with Fitzgerald and a lifestyle that is nonchalant and amoral, or at least nonmoral. The Roaring Twenties were cool; in fact, it was the era in which coolness emerged as a defining trait of youth culture.

Alongside the literature of the Lost Generation, two art movements emerged that also captured the improvisational, transgressive, and break-away character of the Roaring Twenties—and indeed portrayed it visually—Dada and Futurism. The mammoth sculpture by artist Marcel Duchamp, *The Bride Stripped Bare by Her Bachelors, Even*—a work that

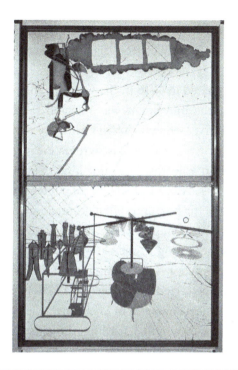

Photo 1.4: Marcel Duchamp's *The Bride Stripped Bare by Her Bachelors, Even* **(1915–1923)**

Source: © Association Marcel Duchamp / ADAGP, Paris / SODRAC, Montréal (2017)

---

defies any simple or singular interpretation—encapsulates the Dadaist style and its view (literally) of the emerging decadent life that besieged both Europe and America. Duchamp's works involved mass-produced objects selected at random and displayed as works of art, and, although he was not technically a Dadaist, he was working in the Dada spirit as early as 1913.

Dadaist art reflected the rise of modern incoherent, spur-of-the-moment, affluent, and bored culture that, to cure its ennui, resorted to a pleasure-based lifestyle and consumption. The Dadaists mirrored the inanity, yet excitement, of the new world order, with its disconnected moral structure and commodity-based worldview, wherein everything from actual goods to art are conceived and distributed as if they were of equal value.

Dada originated in 1916 in the Cabaret Voltaire in Zurich. The word for the movement was selected randomly from a French dictionary. Dada was at first a literary movement based on randomness; the early Dadaist writers created texts from a random selection of words. The same kind of approach was adopted by the artists. So, a Dadaist might put torn pieces of paper into a box, shake the box, and spill its content out onto a sheet of paper; the resulting configuration of the pieces would be collated or even drawn according to the pattern in which they fell. The Dadaists were provocative, and, in a sense, the first youth culture can be characterized as Dadaesque. Dada assumed its most radical and political character in Germany, where World War I had led to severe economic hardship. The appearance of Dada in Paris led to the development of surrealism, another protest movement in the arts, in 1924.

The German poet Richard Huelsenbeck perceptively characterized the Dada movement as follows:

> Dada hurts. Dada does not jest, for the reason that it was experienced by revolutionary men and not by philistines who demand that art be a decoration for the mendacity of their own emotions. I am firmly convinced that all art will become Dadaistic in the course of time, because from Dada proceeds the perpetual urge for its renovation.[24]

Indeed, the feeling of renovation and reinvention is at the core of the social ethos that spawned the Roaring Twenties.

Another movement that prefigured and predicted the free spirit of the era was Futurism, an Italian art movement that flourished from 1909 to about 1916. Futurism glorified the power, speed, and excitement that characterized the emerging machine age—based on the technology of the automobile and of automated manufacturing. From the French Cubist painters and multiple-exposure photography, the Futurists learned to break up realistic forms into multiple images and overlapping fragments of colour. By such means, they attempted to portray the energy and pastiche of modern life.

The Lost Generation, Dadaism, Futurism, and other movements came forward to define the form and spirit of the Roaring Twenties. Although none of these artists directly targeted the reasons for the rise of youth culture, except perhaps Fitzgerald and his essays on flappers, they provided, all together, a rather probing portrait—narrative and figurative—of the era and the psychic reasons for its crystallization. The themes of technology, urbanization, and the quest for pleasure in an age of moral decline are imprinted in their works. All were young people when their writing and art truly mattered.

EPILOGUE

To conclude this chapter, a few highlights can be reiterated here, since these can be considered to be the elements that went into the formation, constitution, and rise of youth culture. In brief, the construction of adolescence, the spread of affluence, urbanization, mass media technologies, and a desire to break away from repressive and suffocating Victorian moralism all converged to spark the early youth movement. The artistic and social ingredients in this movement included jazz music and openly sexual lifestyles, including clothing, night-time parties at speakeasies, cigarettes, and booze—all of which were the target of Prohibition, which only helped spread the flames further and deeper. Anything that is forbidden seems to achieve the opposite result.

The Great Depression of 1929 put a damper on the pleasure-seeking denizens of the new world order, but the fun and excitement was reignited in the 1930s and early 1940s with the

Swing Era—an extension of the Jazz Era. The youth-based lifestyles came to an abrupt end, however, with World War II.

The Roaring Twenties were chronicled and portrayed by writers and artists, such as Fitzgerald, Hemingway, and the Dadaists. The world was changing profoundly, moving away from its largely puritanical past to a freer secular future. The artists and writers saw this, becoming the first to both praise the change and also issue a warning. Perhaps the greatest force propelling forth a veritable youth culture was jazz. Over the history of youth culture, music preferences have become increasingly eclectic. Whatever the style, music has great significance to young people, because it speaks to them emotionally. The ancient philosophers of Classical Greece believed that music originated with the gods Apollo and Orpheus and that it reflected the laws of harmony that rule the universe. They also believed that music influences human thoughts and actions, because each melody possesses an emotional quality that listeners experience directly. In some African societies, music is considered to be the faculty that sets humans apart from other species. Among some Native American cultures, it is thought to have originated as a way for spirits to communicate with human beings.

The question of what constitutes musical art is not an easy one to answer. One thing is for certain: only those works that are genuinely meaningful to one and all will remain. Beethoven's *Missa Solemnis* and his last four string quartets, to mention but two examples, will remain because they convey a profound inner quest for meaning to life. Much of popular music will not. As popular music critic Greil Marcus put it, in the end such music will fade away because it "is a combination of good ideas dried up by fads, terrible junk, hideous failings in taste and judgment, gullibility and manipulation, moments of unbelievable clarity and invention, pleasure, fun, vulgarity, excess, novelty and utter enervation."[25]

All this might sound elitist. But it is not. Mozart wrote music that he intended for the enjoyment of common folk—not just the cognoscenti. The operas of Verdi and Rossini, too, were highly popular. The idea of "classical music" as an elitist form of art is a modern one. And it is a myth. Musical art cannot be easily managed by the entrepreneurs of taste. It will exist regardless of the economic system in place in a given society. It is also ironic to reflect on the fact that the greatest composers of all time were barely "teenagers" when they composed some of their greatest works. And they died at ages that would be considered way too young. To wit: Mozart died at the age of 35, Chopin at 39, and Schubert at 31. But their music was and continues to be "ageless" and "timeless."

Now, most of the early jazz works have gone by the wayside. But there are some that have as much aesthetic validity as do the great works of classical music. Certainly George Gershwin, as mentioned, understood the aesthetic power of jazz. André Previn, who was both a jazz and classical musician, gives the following relevant assessment:

> The basic difference between classical music and jazz is that in the former the music is always greater than its performance—Beethoven's Violin Concerto, for instance, is always greater than its performance—whereas the way jazz is performed is always more important than what is being performed.[26]

CHAPTER 2

Rebirth and Rebellion: The 1950s

The fifties—they seem to have taken place on a sunny afternoon that asked nothing of you except a drifting belief in the
moment and its power to satisfy.

—*Elizabeth Hardwick (1916–2007)*

PROLOGUE

To sustain a youth movement, affluence is required, along-side the mass media to spread it broadly, thereby installing it into groupthink. Money, newness, technology, and lifestyle go hand in hand. When any one of these is lacking, such as during an economic depression or wartime, then the social prerogative of a separate youth-based culture fades into the background. Poverty and war are its antidotes. The budding flapper culture was built on an unprecedented prosperity for virtually everyone after World War I along with the ever-expanding thrust towards urbanization; it thrived and made an indelible impact on society until it was halted by two major events, both of which weakened the affluence levels in America—the Great Depression and World War II. These temporarily made America poorer and more "mature," so to speak, relegating youth lifestyles to its margins. But the Roaring Twenties nevertheless had left their mark on America's cultural DNA—the verve and excitement of the flappers had simply become dormant, waiting for World War II to end and a second wave of general affluence to bring about their rebirth.

It was, in fact, after World War II that a new youthful collective energy fomented in North America. Whereas 1923 can be identified as an originating point for the first generation of youth culture, 1956 can be singled out as a tipping point for the advent of a second major form of youth culture. That was the year that a young Southern singer named Elvis Presley came out of nowhere to record, with a small label, a song called "Heartbreak Hotel." It became an unexpected overnight hit, much like the Charleston in 1923. It was, in retrospect, the founding musical manifesto that heralded a rebirth of youth culture based on the genre of music that the hit song championed—*rock and roll*. Whereas the flappers and flaming youth were a loosely organized group of young people, the followers of Elvis Presley became highly united socially and culturally because of the increasing technologization of the modern world. Indeed, the new rock and roll culture quickly spread through radio hit parades, television programs, films, and concert performances, unifying teenagers everywhere in a quasi-tribal way. The post-war generation saw an unprecedented increase in the birth rate of babies—hence their characterization as *baby boomers*. By the mid-1950s many were approaching puberty. Thus, a "perfect storm" of events—new levels of affluence, peacetime, technology, the growth of mass media, a huge and growing demographic of young people—had occurred that led to the establishment of a vibrant and powerful new form of youth culture.

The word *teenager* became a common one throughout society at the time to describe the arrival of this demographic.[1] Over the years that term has changed its meaning, or at least its nuances, a fact that suggests how language is a history-documenting device for mutations in culture. But the image, or caricature, that it evokes remains a linguistic time capsule of a young person in the rock and roll era. Teenagers walked, talked, and always looked "cool," setting themselves visibly apart from adults. An adolescent is allowed to be awkward; a teenager is not—or at least *was* not in the 1950s. The teenager was also pegged a "social rebel" for the first time in history.

The 1950s teenagers did not invent rebellion, of course. The flappers and flaming youth of the 1920s, along with the Lost Generation writers, were rebels in the sense that their rebellion was social and artistic, rather than military. But no one named them as such. The youths who created and engaged in the emerging rock and roll culture were, in effect, seen as "rebels without a (political) cause," as the iconic movie of that era starring James Dean proclaimed; the youths who spearheaded the subsequent counterculture of the 1960s, on the other hand, engaged in a more political and subversive form of rebellion. Behind the rebellion, imagined or real, is the music.

Why rebel? Against what, in an affluent world, or at least in a world where meals will be provided even to poor people who ask for them? Unlike developing or poorer countries, most of the Western world has never really had to go to bed necessarily or unavoidably hungry. The rebellion, therefore, was not a socioeconomically motivated one—in either the Roaring Twenties or the 1950s. Arguably, it was, and continues to be, a rebellion against the ennui of modern life—a situation that also sparked the nihilistic, existentialist, and postmodern movements at one level and the fun-loving rock and roll culture at another.

Some sociologists in the first half of the twentieth century saw the source of ennui as rampant capitalism and its petty bourgeois worldview, which revolves around humdrum and tedious habits in everyday life—at the time called the "assembly line" society. French philosopher Marcel Mauss, for example, saw people living in capitalist systems as automatons thrust into meaningless habits by those in the upper echelons of society who lived by the profit motive.[2] Social success depends, therefore, largely on an individual's ability to absorb the habits of society, even if they lead to mindless behaviour. This whole line of thought derives ultimately from the notion of *alienation*—a term coined by Karl Marx to describe a sensed estrangement from other people or work that he claimed was endemic to capitalist societies, which he described as shallow and depersonalizing.[3] Sociologist Émile Durkheim, on the other hand, argued that alienation stemmed from a loss of moral and religious traditions, not from capitalism itself.[4] He used the term *anomie* to refer to the sense of irrational boredom and purposelessness experienced by a person or a class resulting from a lack of moral imperatives or goals to be achieved. Anomie may, in fact, be *the* unconscious factor that spurred on youth rebellion in the twentieth century. This is a topic that would require a separate treatment, though. Suffice it to say here that it may not be far-fetched to envision anomie and ennui as potential sources of rebellion among young people against the status quo.

The 1950s teenagers were rebelling, in effect, against a social system that had become stale, dull, monotonous, and unimaginative—a world that saw blandness as the norm. Feeling a disjunction between themselves and this norm, the teenagers rebelled in their own way. They did so by adopting a new music and lifestyle of their own *en masse*, in exactly the same way that the youth of the Roaring Twenties had done. The world had entered the Rock Era, which was in many ways an extension or natural outgrowth of the Jazz Era—just the musical details were different, but not unrelated or discontinuous. The media picked up on the emerging situation opportunely, promoting the musical rebellion massively through records, movies, magazines, radio, and television. Rebellion had become big business—a strange and paradoxical partnership indeed.

But the rebellion was not only a symptom of the reaction against boredom—a symptom of affluent, spoiled young people with nothing better to do. As it turned out, it constituted an unconscious quest for social justice and for attacking hypocrisy in social mores. The teenagers of the 1950s could easily identify the many injustices and hypocritical attitudes that existed in society. Sex, for example, was kept hidden and out of sight, even though it went on all the time—"around the clock" as Bill Haley & His Comets put it in their iconic 1954 song, "Rock Around the Clock." The "rock rebels" revolted against this very type of hypocrisy—the same type against which the flappers had rebelled. It seems that, as the French expression goes, *plus ça change, plus c'est la même chose.* As in the 1920s, ironically, various taboos were in place with regard to public displays of love and romance that were just as silly as those that brought about Prohibition. The response to the hypocrisy was not overt and blatant. It was subtle. For this reason, even an item like "blue suede shoes" took on great symbolic proportions in the Rock Era. Those types of shoes were seen by adults as too gaudy and inappropriate for young people. So, Carl Perkins defiantly made them the theme of a hit song—"Blue Suede Shoes" (1955). The song made it clear that no one should "step on them."

In short, rebellion in the 1950s was encoded in rock and roll, which entailed a new look (fashion), a new talk (language), and a new walk (attitude). In both the 1920s and 1950s, there was an unconscious need to change the world. And in both eras, the young musicians were both black and white, going against horrific racial barriers. The jarring image of mixed-race performers sharing the same stage and the same limelight brought about a growing debate over racism itself, bringing it out into the open. In other words, the rebellion set the stage for a veritable social, political, and legal revolution.

ELVIS PRESLEY

"When I first heard Elvis's voice I just knew that I wasn't going to work for anybody and nobody was gonna be my boss. Hearing him for the first time was like busting out of jail."[5]

These words were spoken by none other than Bob Dylan, who himself became a symbol of the counterculture movement in the mid-1960s. In it, we can see an insightful acknowledgement of the rebelliousness imprinted in the music of Elvis Presley—the "king" of rock and roll culture.

The critical mass for the Rock Era came in 1956 with Presley's "Heartbreak Hotel," as mentioned. Presley was first heard on American radio on July 7, 1954. From the outset, he was marketed especially to young adolescent females, as a modern-day "sex god." He was Eros in the flesh, bringing about a new perception of the body as a source of rebellion against moral hypocrisy.

Elvis caused moral panic because of his sexual persona and, especially, because of his adoption of African American music. As in the Jazz Era, puritanism and racism had reared their ugly

Photo 2.1: Elvis Presley in 1957

Source: Publicity still for the film *Jailhouse Rock*, courtesy of Wikimedia Commons

heads once again. No wonder that Elvis was attacked by many at first as a harbinger of moral doom. But his perceived threat to society quickly subsided, as the media and the entertainment industries capitalized on his popularity and sex appeal, tapping into a growing sense that youth rebellion was a profitable (if not *the* most profitable) type of rebellion. Elvis was soon re-packaged to become acceptable to a larger public, through radio, television, records, concerts, and movies. Long after his death, "the king" lives on through videos, reissues of his records, brand name products (socks, sweaters, lipstick, pencils, sodas, pyjamas, etc.), imitators who continue on where the real Elvis left off, and the establishment of the Graceland museum in Memphis.

In 1968, believing that the music world was passing him by, as the Rock Era was coming to an end, Elvis attempted a come-back on television—the most powerful medium at the time. The program, known subsequently as Elvis's "Comeback Special," was such a hit that it encouraged him to resume touring and to embark on new recording ventures, producing hit songs such as "Burning Love" (1969) and "Suspicious Minds" (1969). As a result, his audience broadened to include older and diverse fans. Presley also took up performing regularly in Las Vegas in 1969, becoming an enormous success there, but with adult, not adolescent, audiences. Throughout the early 1970s he regained some of his previous regal status, but not on account of the new generation of young people, who saw him as a caricature of his previous self. In fact, the garish and ostentatious white costume that he donned at his performances was more reminiscent of the glitzy costumes of street minstrels than of a rock star hero. To those who cared about his music, all this was seen as the tragic descent of a fallen hero; the new generation of teenagers saw it instead as cartoonish burlesque. Indeed, they saw the whole 1950s movement as superficial, shallow, and insignificant—an erroneous knee-jerk reaction that has remained constant virtu-ally to this day.

Elvis was keenly aware of his unfortunate predicament. And, in fact, the pressures of being the previous king of rock and roll took their toll. Like a mythic god who has fallen from favour, his last years were beset by tragedy. He died at his home in Memphis, at the age of 42. Like a mythic figure, Presley became even more celebrated after his death, with the devotion of his fans becoming religious in intensity early on. Although this faded considerably at the start of the twenty-first century, it brings out the fact that each era of youth culture tends to morph into a highly nostalgic one after the fact. The story of Elvis is, actually, a story of how youth culture comes and goes, much like a commodity, as the Marxist scholars have perhaps correctly asserted. To this day, Graceland—Elvis's home in Memphis—is still an international tourist attraction, to which people around the world make a pilgrimage of sorts, especially on the anniversary of his death of a drug overdose on August 16, 1977. But all such pilgrimages evoke today is nostalgia.

There is little doubt that Elvis would not have been deified without the type of music he championed—rock and roll. Early 1950s rock was a huge success among young people, because it literally "rocked and rolled" them. Television jumped on the bandwagon, further entrenching its appeal. On August 5, 1957, *American Bandstand* came on American television to more than eight million viewers. The show tapped perfectly into the emerging youth emotional rhythms, desires, and tastes. The response was overwhelming. It swept across American adolescence like a cultural meme, as it would be called today. The announcer, Dick Clark, became himself an icon, remaining so until his death in 2012. The program aired in the late afternoon, after school, so as to allow hordes of teenagers to gather around the TV screen not only to keep up with the new songs and artists but also to participate in an imaginary community of social peers. Knowing what new songs were "in" through the program constituted crucial information to those who wanted to be an intrinsic part of the community.

The Elvis Presley phenomenon was a veritable watershed one in the history of youth culture. The Roaring Twenties really did not have a singular hero in the same way, nor did subsequent youth movements. Elvis's music, performance style, and perceived sexual rebelliousness—he was called "Elvis the Pelvis" because he shook his hips in a sexually suggestive manner—turned the page on how youth culture has been perceived ever since. There have been subsequent "rock stars," but virtually no one among the mix could be raised to the level of a "king of rock and roll," perhaps because rock and roll died in the late 1950s, with subsequent forms of the music evolving in different aesthetic directions. During his childhood, Presley was exposed to the genre of music that shaped his singing style, namely, the blues and gospel music of African Americans. He absorbed it profoundly and became one of its greatest unwitting promoters through his own stylistic adaptations. He has often been called a "white African American" for this very reason. In 1953, at the age of 18, he made his first record by paying the Memphis Recording Service to record two songs. The owner, Sam Phillips, was so impressed by his singing, and, more importantly, by his debonair handsome looks, that he called Elvis back the following year to record for Sun Records. His 1954 song, "That's All Right," became a local hit. The Elvis Presley phenomenon had arrived.

Presley started recording for national labels in 1956. On September 9 of that year, a record number of television viewers watched him perform on the *Ed Sullivan Show* on CBS—the most watched program on Sunday evenings. He became an instant nationwide celebrity, not just a teen rock star. His early hits—"Heartbreak Hotel" (1956), "Don't Be Cruel" (1956), "Love Me Tender" (1956), "All Shook Up" (1957), "Teddy Bear" (1957), "Loving You" (1957), "Jailhouse Rock" (1957), "It's Now or Never" (1960)—are still being performed and loved by those who discover them today. They signalled the arrival of a new genre of music that was exciting in its fast tempo versions and haunting in its ballad form. Adults had a hard time accepting him; many simply thought of him as an anomaly who would soon disappear, but many others saw him as the devil incarnate. What was this world coming to, thought the latter, with someone like Presley shaking his pelvis on stage? It was, in fact, his body moves in particular that aroused a storm of criticism. Some cities and towns banned his concerts, and refused to play his records on radio. A few performers even refused to appear on the same stage with him. But all this did not matter to the teens of the era. They saw his stage act as exciting, rebellious, and just plain fun. The females in the audience shrieked, yelled, swooned, and even shed tears, being so powerfully moved by the blatant sexuality of his act. Rock music historian Nick Johnstone summarizes the impact of Elvis's stage persona aptly as follows:

> Live, Elvis would get up there and move. Not just shake a leg or snap his fingers, but dance. Really dance, wiggle his hips, shake his pelvis and leap about. The girls would go crazy. Here he was, this good-looking Memphis boy with his greased back hair, sideburns, flamboyant clothes (for instance, black trousers with a pink stripe up the leg) and wild moves. He'd come out on stage and spit. Address them in the rough and tumble vernacular of his upbringing, his recent work as a truck driver. Stand there, in silence, chewing gum, the whole crowd in the palm of his hand, wondering what's he going to do next, and they loved it. His performance spoke of sex too. Oozed sex, reeked of sex, promised sex at a time when no performer was permitted to speak of sex in any way. But now, here he was: on stage, wiggling his pelvis lasciviously while Mick Jagger was over in England, still a child.[6]

Elvis was youth culture's first "bad boy." It is little wonder that his film *Jailhouse Rock* (1957) had him singing from a prison at one point in the movie—a powerful, transgressive portrait of the bad boy in the pre-rap era. The devotion of his fans at the time reached high levels of loyalty and enthusiasm. Below the radar, rock and roll was yet another testament to the importance of African American culture to America. Its champion in the 1950s was Elvis Presley.

REBELLION

Rock and roll had two sides to it. First, there were the hard-driving rock songs by Little Richard, Bill Haley & His Comets, Carl Perkins, and others; alongside these there were the more romantic ballads by iconic groups like the Platters and the Drifters. The subject matter of these songs reflected the lives and emotions of teens in the era. They also documented the presence of implicit rituals among young people, including coming-of-age ones. Sixteen was the year pegged to constitute the "end of adolescence"—the age at which teenagers were expected to graduate from high school. Rock tunes with titles such as "Sixteen Candles" and "Sweet Little Sixteen" became the ritualistic chants of this new *sui generis* passage rite. Rituals (even informal ad hoc ones) allow groups to understand themselves and their relationship to the world around them. Ritualizing such events as the sixteenth birthday through songs and other ceremonial activities allowed teens in the 1950s to share common experiences. However, unlike religious or other formal rituals, they were ephemeral and subject to change from one teen generation to the next. Indeed, the sixteenth birthday party virtually disappeared as a ritual in the next generation of teens.

The 1950s, like the 1920s, was an exciting new time for everyone, even those who denounced rock and roll and its attendant lifestyle. The persona of the teenager became embedded in the broader social landscape. It was inscribed there through the media, record companies, film studios, television channels, and new special magazines. Many sectors of the postwar economy became, in fact, highly dependent on the buying power of adolescents. The rebellion was a convenient one for the marketplace. The baby boomer teens were probably the first generation to have a great deal of leisure time and much more money at their disposal than teens in previous eras of America. They showed a propensity to consume and spend on rock and roll records and related lifestyle paraphernalia. Television dance programs—the forerunners of MTV—made instant celebrities of the teenage dancers who performed on them. As culture theorists Jane and Michael Stern have eloquently put it, the world of the 1950s "was for teens only; and it heralded the arrival of a new generation eager to embrace a pop culture of its own."[7] Youth culture had become an overarching reality, in the marketplace, in the media, and in the collective imagination. As youth culture analyst Thomas Doherty has put it,

> At once socially special and specially socialized, '50s teenagers experienced the same things together—through their assigned place in the burgeoning consumer economy, in the increasing uniformity of public school education throughout the states, and in the national media that doted on their idiosyncrasies.[8]

The common experiences were embedded in rock and roll, which was tamed considerably in the early 1960s to become more broadly acceptable.

Following in Elvis's footsteps were a host of "lesser gods" who also vied for mythic status among teens. Jerry Lee Lewis, for instance, further extended the sexual innuendoes of Elvis's "All Shook Up" (1956) with such hits as "Whole Lotta Shakin'

Goin' On" (1957), "Great Balls of Fire" (1958), and "Breathless" (1958). If Elvis was Apollo, Lewis was Dionysus. Lewis thrilled teens and horrified parents. But the panic was not to continue for very long, as television turned "softer" rock stars like Ricky Nelson, one of the Nelson teens on the popular sitcom *The Adventures of Ozzie and Harriet*, into overnight successes—thus taming the beast in rock and roll, so to speak. Incidentally, that sitcom was one of the first to deal specifically with the problems of raising adolescent children in the post-war era. Well-groomed male rock teen idols such as Frankie Avalon, Fabian, Paul Anka, and Bobby Rydell, with their softer sound (contrasting with the hard-driving sound of Chuck Berry or Little Richard), were instant success stories. By the end of the 1950s, youth culture was developing a "split personality." Elvis was still around, but he was losing his supremacy and his raw edge. The new breed of rock idols performed a toned-down and more socially acceptable version of rock and roll. The allegiance of teens waffled from one to the other. The actor James Dean embodied both sides of this split personality. Physically, he resembled one of the new docile teen stars, well-groomed and mild-mannered. But below this veneer, he exuded the rebelliousness and sexuality of Elvis. James Dean was both Elvis Presley and Ricky Nelson wrapped into one.

As the movie *Hairspray* by John Waters brought out, the rebellion started by the Rock Era rockers and stars was an unwitting one. It happened on its own, uniting races and genders in the cauldron of excitement that was rock and roll. The 2007 version of the movie revisited the end-of-the-50s and early-60s era in a musical and lighthearted yet perceptive way, even though the original 1988 version was much more satirical of the era itself. But the subtext of the movie is undeniable—the 1950s made a difference, even if often the era is criticized as superficial. The rebellion was not out in the open, but it was still there, lurking just below the surface and waiting to come out in full force.

Photo 2.2: James Dean (1955)

Source: Publicity still for the film *Rebel without a Cause*, courtesy of Wikimedia Commons

COOLNESS

In a perceptive moment of reflection, the acerbic writer Norman Mailer made the following statement with regard to the rebelliousness introduced into society by young people:

> One is Hip or one is Square, one is a rebel or one conforms, one is a frontiersman in Wild West of American night life, or else a Square cell, trapped in the totalitarian tissues of American society, doomed willy-nilly to conform if one is to succeed.[9]

As Steven Quartz and Anette Asp comment in their perceptive book, *Cool,* the socially constructed figure of the young rebel is indeed full of contrasts and ambiguities; interestingly, they compare the figure of the rebel teen to the image of the psychopath: "He is a radical nonconformist who is violent, a sexual outlaw, amoral, and unencumbered by conscience."[10]

Followers of Elvis and the whole rock scene that sprouted up around him welcomed the psychopathy of the moment—a chance to live differently through the abrasiveness of rock and roll. Coolness was the code of the rocker. This meant crafting the right look and utilizing the right talk, listening to the right music, and hanging out with the right friends at "joints" such as diners—there were no malls then. Cars also played a significant role in the whole coolness thing—driving one, souping it up, and using it as a sign of both maturity and independence. This was brought out brilliantly by the movie *Grease* (1978). The male rocker's appearance, epitomized by both Elvis and James Dean, became symbolic of the silent rebellion that was unfolding; it was a way of communicating rebellious "coolness" through dress, hairstyle (including sideburns and slick hair), slang, and a general demeanour that implicitly conveyed badness. Female rockers developed two kinds of cool looks—one that was "hard," as represented by the wearing of tight pants, à la Connie Francis, and one that was "soft," as represented instead by the wearing of poodle skirts and bobby socks. It is no coincidence that psychologists started to study body image in the 1950s as a defining feature of adolescent personality and as a key to understanding problematic adolescent behaviours.

But the psychologist's notion of body image is not all there was to the story of the early rockers. In its own way, their "redesign" of the body to fit a self-styled coolness model was implicitly confrontational—"psychopathic," to use Quartz and Asp's analogy. It flew in the face of the adult world of stodgy grey flannel suits, ties, long skirts, prim and proper hair, and so on. The rocker code stood clearly apart from that world. And it got the reaction it was designed to evoke. The adults saw rock and roll as a symptom of moral decay. But it was hardly that. It communicated a tacit rebellion—a rebellion against the adults through symbolic lifestyles that set the teens apart from other age groups.

Some psychologists would claim that codes such as the rocker one are used to hide or attenuate the fear teens feel about body image. There is some truth to this. Because different parts of the body grow at different rates during puberty, many adolescents temporarily look and feel awkward, and this sense of awkwardness may make them apprehensive about the way they look. The code allows teens to attenuate their emotional states, rendering them harmless through a performance of coolness. Song titles of the era such as "Lonely Boy," "It's Only Make Believe," "Rock Around the Clock," "A Teenager in Love," "Crying," and "Little Runaway," among many others, constituted a psycho-discography of contrasting adolescent emotions and views of the world.

The code also started a second revolution in gender relations— the first one being the flapper code, as we saw. Until the 1950s, men were expected to be the sex seekers, to initiate courtship, and to show a general aggressive interest in females. But with girl groups like Martha and the Vandellas and their gender-role-bashing songs, like "Heat Wave," "Nowhere to Run," and "Jimmy Mack," women were fashioning a new independent sexual voice for themselves, a voice that said: "I'll choose the man that I want, on my own terms." They were the new flappers.[11] Young women started to move away from seeing themselves primarily as housewives of the future, as in the popular TV sitcom *Father Knows Best* (which began in 1949 on radio). A new world order was just around the corner. The female rock artist came to symbolize a young independent woman who found her identity in herself, not in the models of society. She became a critical cog in an extraordinary social movement that has profoundly changed the way we look at marriage and the family. As writer Ursula K. Le Guin has aptly phrased it, the feminine principle, as she called it, "is, or at least historically has been, basically anarchic. It values order without constraint, rule by custom not by force. It has been the male who enforces order, who constructs power structures, who makes, enforces, and breaks laws."[12]

It would, of course, be incorrect to say that the same pattern of change has become a universal one across the world. And even in America, it is still somewhat of a struggle for women to gain independence from the patriarchal past. All that can be said here is that women's liberation has been unfolding gradually through decades of struggles.[13] Misogyny can still be found everywhere in modern societies, but it started to be exposed as unacceptable in the youth cultures of the 1920s and 1950s.

Coolness was, as suggested above, a quiet form of rebellion against the status quo—a rebellion imprinted in clothes, body image, and attitude, not in any overt confrontational discourse. As journalist John Leland has argued, it is really a version of a more general form of insubordinate behaviour that was called *hip* in early America.[14] He dates the coinage of that word to 1619, the year when the first blacks arrived in America off the coast of Virginia. Without black culture, and its music, Leland maintains, there would be no hip or cool culture today. The word comes from two West African Wolof verbs: *hepi*, meaning "to see" and *hipi*, meaning "to open one's eyes." Hip is all about getting people to open their eyes to see the "attitude" imprinted in the walk, the talk, and the look of a hipster. Hip is something that you can feel and see rather than understand. It has always been associated with musical styles—especially jazz and rock. In its 1973 anthem tune, the funk group Tower of Power characterized hipness as follows: "Hipness is—What it is! And sometimes hipness is, what it ain't." Hip and cool are all about a flight from conformity, a way to put oneself in contrast to it, to stand out, to look and be different. Leland quips that Bugs Bunny, the loveable cartoon character, exemplified hipness, with his sassy attitude that always got the better of Elmer Fudd, the ultimate "square." Bugs's "What's up, Doc?" is pure hip talk. It is no coincidence that the same verbal expression became a part of hip-hop slang ("Whassup?") in the 1990s. Bugs was so hip, Leland goes on to say, that sometimes he even stopped in the middle of a cartoon to argue with his human creators.

There are, however, downsides to coolness. The inability to present an appropriate cool persona can have rather dire consequences, even if the inability is just an imagined one. The increase in eating disorders in the 1950s was one of these. Sociologists have reported that today even prepubescent girls are often worried about being overweight. "Appearance junkies," as writer Emily White calls them, are made, not born.[15] Cigarette smoking was, and probably still is to some extent, also a downside. It was an intrinsic part of acting cool. It constituted a symbolic prop that blurted out, "I am smoking in the face of reprobation. I am cool."

But on the other side of the coin, coolness also had a hidden therapeutic effect—it allowed teenagers to cope with adolescent life. Coolness was a therapeutic philosophy of life, a response to a deep need to come to grips consciously with the overwhelming structure of the world at puberty. Coolness was (and still is) a way to divest the structure of its emotional stranglehold over young people.

Slang also became an integral part of the code. Knowing the right words, turns of phrase, and expressions holds great social power among peers.[16] Words such as *chick* ("young, attractive female"), *jock* ("muscular male teen who is a sports star at school"), and *cat* ("cool male teen"), for example, became part of a lexicon of coolness. Interestingly, some of these have become so much a part of our everyday vocabulary that we no longer remember that they originated in 1950s slang. Slang appeals because it is brash and rebellious, and it knocks down grammatical and prescriptive traditions, which are felt to be vacuous and superficial. As the American author and critic Elizabeth Hardwick so astutely observed,

> The language of the younger generation has the brutality of the city and an assertion of threatening power at hand. It is military, theatrical, and at its most coherent probably a lasting repudiation of empty courtesy and bureaucratic euphemism.[17]

THE ROCK ERA

"Rock music should be gross: that's the fun of it. It gets up and drops its trousers."[18] These words were uttered by British rock guitarist Bruce Dickinson. They encapsulate what rock and roll was essentially all about—fun, tracing its roots ultimately to jazz and the fun that it too engendered in the 1920s. It took elements of boogie-woogie, doo-wop, honky-tonk, blues, and gospel, fusing them in such a way as to create a new genre— a musical compound that was greater than the sum of its parts.

A rock song such as "Heartbreak Hotel" swings in basic jazz–bebop style; but one can also clearly hear in it elements of blues, gospel, country, and hillbilly music.

The first rock songs were recorded and released by small, independent record companies and promoted by controversial radio disc jockeys such as Alan Freed, who used the term *rock and roll* to help attract white audiences who were generally unfamiliar with African American music styles. Some critics attribute the origin of the term to Freed himself, but it was already used by the Boswell Sisters in their 1934 song titled "Rock and Roll," although their term referred to the back-and-forth movement of a rocking chair in that song, not to the meanings it eventually developed in rock culture. The origin of the term is explained by Nick Johnstone as follows:

> Myth has it that Freed lifted the term 'rock 'n' roll' from a lyric in the over brag of sexual potency that is the 1951 rhythm and blues hit, "Sixty Minute Man," by African-American vocal group The Dominoes (the rapper Missy Elliott later responded with a female comeback to the make brag in 2001 with the song, "One Minute Man"). He reappropriated the lyric off the cuff on air and a catchphrase was born. Within a few shows, Freed was known for playing rock 'n' roll music. Safe in the knowledge that the show was a hit and the station no longer had any grounds to fire him for potentially drawing the station into controversy, he went all the way and announced to listeners that his show was from now on going to go out under the name *The Moondog Rock 'n' Roll Party.*[19]

By the time Elvis Presley recorded "Good Rockin' Tonight" in 1954, which was a remake of Wynonie Harris's 1948 rendition of the song, rock and roll had arrived on the scene as a powerful new music. After Bill Haley & His Comets recorded

"Rock Around the Clock" in 1955, it quickly became the musical voice that teenagers came to call exclusively theirs. The latter song was the theme music for *The Blackboard Jungle*, a 1955 motion picture about teenagers. It was the first in the coming-of-age filmic genre that continues to have success to this day.

By 1956, rock had established itself firmly and loudly (some would say) across America and Europe. Johnstone puts it in the following perceptive and eloquent way:

> So, 1956 was *the* rock 'n' roll year, the year in which popular music history had its greatest musical upheaval, revolution and transformation. In the events of that one year, music changed the landscape of the world in a way it hadn't before and hasn't since. It blew up as a youth movement, riding the then novel emerging adolescent culture and in giving voice to a mass dissatisfaction with the status quo, and in doing so called for a new way of living. It was a reflection of a changing world, an expression of the post-Second World War American landscape. The axis was shifting as the first cracks appeared, Elvis turned up, the right man in the right place at the right time. Some people say if Elvis hadn't come along to light the fuse, then another artist would have done it. Not true. It happened exactly the way it was meant to happen. No other artist at the time had the potential to take rock 'n' roll so far, so high, so fast. And in that one year, Elvis Presley turned the world upside down and reset the cultural face of American music, all music. Yes, punk, hip hop and grunge all later brought their own mini-youth revolutions, made their mark in the way we live, the way we talk, the way we think, but not on the scale in which Elvis Presley et al stormed charts and minds in 1956.[20]

As rock and roll spread, it allowed teenagers throughout the nation, and indeed the world, to feel that they were part of

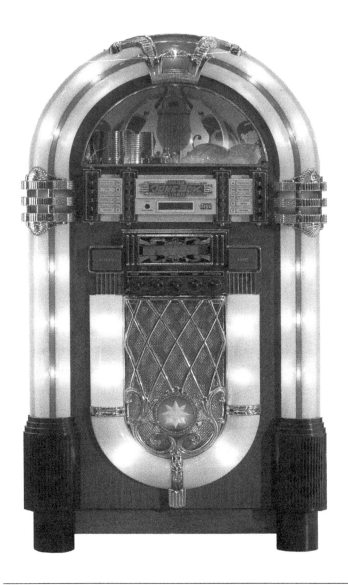

Photo 2.3: A 1950s Jukebox

something cool and exciting. The jukebox became a symbol of this new mood and so requires a brief commentary here. It was invented in 1906. By the early 1950s, most restaurants and diners had one. The jukeboxes typically featured current rock and roll hits. The 1970s TV sitcom *Happy Days* brought out the symbolic importance of this machine. After school, the adolescents in the sitcom congregated in a diner that featured a jukebox, which blurted out rock tunes. This put the characters in a frame of mind to interact socially and romantically. In other words, it functioned as a magnet around which the teenagers congregated to ritualize their friendship (or lack thereof) together. In the 1953 movie *The Wild One* the meaning of the jukebox as a symbol of teen rebellion was emphasized in the scene where Marlon Brando, the protagonist motorcycle rider, is seen near one. He is asked by the diner owner, who recognized the menacing bad boy image that Brando exuded, "What are you rebelling against?" Brando's answer quickly became a rallying cry for teens, as he drummed his fingers on the jukebox: "Whaddaya got?" By the 1960s, the jukeboxes became more a part of memorabilia than anything else. But in the 1950s, the jukebox was a social experience in itself.

Aware of the power of rock and roll, Hollywood jumped on the bandwagon, producing, in addition to *The Blackboard Jungle* and *Rebel without a Cause*, a slew of rock movies that were forerunners of the music video. The 1956 movie *Rock, Rock, Rock*, for instance, included acts by the leading rock musicians and groups of the era. It also featured an appearance by Alan Freed. Similarly, in *Rock, Baby, Rock It* (1957) and *Go, Johnny, Go!* (1958), the finest musical talent of the era was featured. The rock stars became emblazoned on the screen, increasing the level of idolatry that they garnered from their fans.

The simplest rock and roll piece relies on a basic beat and a few chord progressions. But in its structural simplicity, it somehow allows for a wide range of emotions and ideas to be expressed. The songs dealt with such themes as cars, girls, boys, the heartbreak of romance, the promise of sex, and the joy of being young. Rock and roll dances, known as *sock hops*, became part of teenage life. Every teenager was expected to go to these, which were held typically in the high school gymnasium, where the dancers were required to remove their shoes to protect the floor from scratches, scuffs, and scrapes—hence the term *sock hop*. Those who went were called "cats" and "dolls"; those who did not were seen as socially marginalized. As Little Richard put it in his 1956 song "Ready Teddy," "All the flattop cats and the dungaree dolls/Are headed to the gym for the sock hop ball." Dance crazes like the stroll and the hop emerged in this social milieu. They were the descendants of the youthful spirit associated with the Charleston.

Rock and roll dancing was all about the body in motion— swinging the female body around the dance floor and, thus, putting it tantalizingly on display. In some dance crazes, like the Twist, partners did not touch each other while they danced; they "twisted" their legs in tempo to the music. It was, nevertheless, very enticing and seductive, a rock and roll version of the classic *pas de deux*. The dancing was free-spirited and fun, allowing the dancers to create their own moves spontaneously. The association of rock dancing to corporeality has been eloquently highlighted by culture theorist Lawrence Grossberg as follows:

> The body of youth in rock was always a body on display, to others and itself, as the mark of a celebration of energy and fun. They mattered because they were at the heart of rock, and rock mattered. Rock touched, fragmented, multiplied, propelled the bodies of its fans. It created a transitory body which was put into place against the various emotional narratives and alienating experiences of youth's everyday lives.[21]

Needless to say, the dancing was seen as indecent, coarse, and offensive by adults. Who cared what the adults thought?

We will do what we want, answered the teens. But it would not last, giving way to love-ins and happenings in the subsequent hippie era. The rockers danced, the hippies protested instead as they smoked pot.

So, why did the Rock Era come to an end? When Elvis was inducted in the army in 1958, many pundits prognosticated the era's end, making it a very short-lived one, even though the first years of the 1960s saw the arrival of the tamer rock stars, as mentioned, and Elvis's new career as a film star. But the rebellious and abrasive spirit of rock and roll would soon be inherited by a new generation young people who transformed it radically. The hippies were, in fact, just around the corner, ready to take the rebellion in a vastly different direction. Also, paradoxically, rock and roll had become acceptable and enjoyable to the very people who condemned it—the adults. This was a death knell to the era. Finally, the music had become predictable and formulaic. The original verve of the songs of Elvis and Little Richard and the haunting romanticism of the Platters had faded into a set of predictable melodies, harmonies, and rhythms by second-tier artists, who had become much too boring.

In 1956, Danny and the Juniors proclaimed with their hit song that "Rock and Roll Is Here to Stay." As it turned out, that proclamation was only true in part. That is because, in 1964, rock and roll took an unexpected turn. That turn created the next generation of youth culture—as we will see.

BEAT WRITERS AND POP ART

As we saw in the previous chapter, new trends in literature and the arts dovetailed with the rise of flapper culture. The same pattern characterized rock and roll culture. This does not imply that one directly influenced the other. Indeed, very few 1950s teens knew about the work of the Beat writers of their era; similarly, the Beat writers hardly noticed the importance of rock and roll at first. But gradually writers and artists did take notice of the youth culture of the 1950s, as witnessed by the content and style of the works.

In the early part of the 1950s, young writers like Jack Kerouac and Allen Ginsberg came forward with their own form of rebellion. They were labelled the "Beat Generation," an epithet coined by Kerouac himself and one that we still use today. Like Fitzgerald and Hemingway in the 1920s, they also broke from existing literary traditions, emphasizing a new freedom of expression that, in its overall spirit, mirrored the implicit rebellion of the Rock Era. While there is a significant discrepancy between the works of the Beat writers and the early rock songs, there is little doubt that they were implanted on the same emotional substratum—rebellion from the boredom and hypocrisy of adult society. The Beat movement came a few years before the height of the Rock Era; so the writers espoused jazz as their musical idiom of preference. But, eventually they came to understand the emotional power of rock and roll.

The Beat writers were concentrated in San Francisco, Los Angeles, and Greenwich Village in New York City. They held "happenings," which included reading their works combined with jazz, drugs, and open sexuality. Today, they are considered to be the predecessors of the hippies rather than the forerunners of the Rock Era teens; but this is not totally accurate. Their writings expressed the new rebellious *esprit* that was soon to become imprinted in rock and roll—every rock performance in the 1950s was a kind of "happening." The use of alcohol and drugs, and the engagement in sexual activities, were not as open as in the Beat happenings; their use was surreptitious and furtive, but it was there. Boozing and sex usually took place in secret, such as in an automobile late at night or in the home when parents were conveniently away.

Photo 2.4: Jack Kerouac

Source: Phillip Harrington / Alamy Stock Photo

The best known Beat writers were Allen Ginsberg, especially famous for his poem *Howl* (1956), and Jack Kerouac, known for his iconic novel *On the Road* (1957) in which the theme of the journey in youth became a new mythology. Other writers included William S. Burroughs, Gregory Corso, Lawrence Ferlinghetti, and Gary Snyder. Conservative literary critics accused the Beat writers of promoting literary anarchy and obscenity. But others saw their approach as capturing post-war society's growing dissatisfaction with dull conformity and the false values of "square" society. They also advocated for peace and civil rights.

The core group assembled for the first time in 1944 at Columbia University in New York City. Most moved to San Francisco, which became the hub for the happenings in the first half of the 1950s. Interestingly, the writers and their followers were called *hipsters*. Writer Marty Jezer describes the hipster attitude insightfully as follows:

> Their rejection of the commonplace was so complete that they could barely acknowledge reality. The measure of their withdrawal was their distrust of language. A word like *cool* could mean any of a number of contradictory things—its definition came not from the meaning of the word but from the emotion behind it and the accompanying non-verbal facial or body expressions. When hipsters did put together a coherent sentence, it was always prefaced with the word *like* as if to state at the onset that what would follow was probably an illusion.[22]

Prefiguring John Lennon's marvellous 1971 song "Imagine," the Beat Generation saw the world as belonging to one and only one race—the human race. They saw traditional institutions such as religion, the military, government, school, and business as divisive and ultimately destructive. Again, Jezer sums up the hipster philosophy succinctly as follows:

> The hipster's world view was not divided between "free world" and "Communist bloc," and this too set it apart from the then-current orthodoxy. Hipster dualism, instead, transcended geopolitical lines in favor of levels of consciousness. The division was hip and square. Squares sought security and conned themselves into political acquiescence. Hipsters, hip to the bomb, sought the meaning of life and, expecting death, demanded it now. In the wigged-out, flipped-out, zonked-out hipster world, Roosevelt, Churchill, Stalin, Truman, McCarthy and Eisenhower shared one thing in common: they were squares; the hipster signified the coming together of the bohemian, the juvenile delinquent, and the black.[23]

At about the same time, a new art movement surfaced that was also seen as a post-war act of rebellion against the status quo. It came to be called "pop art." Pop art was to the youth culture of the 1950s what Dada was to the youth culture of the Roaring Twenties. Both fit in perfectly with the Zeitgeist of their eras.

The movement took shape principally in the United States and Great Britain. Many of the pop art works were satirical and playful, highlighting the role of everyday commercialism in common people's experience. They represented scenes and objects from within mass consumerist culture, sometimes with actual consumer products (soup cans, comic books, detergents, and the like) as props in the sculptures. In other words, the pop artists sought to depict the reality of everyday life in a consumer-crazy world—a reality characterized by fast-food items, comic-strip frames, celebrities, and the like. The leader of the movement was the American artist Andy Warhol, whose portrait of a Campbell's soup can, in 1964, came to symbolize the whole pop art movement.

Pop artists abandoned individual, titled paintings in favour of works depicting the same object over and over, mirroring the manufacturing process of the assembly line. Warhol carried the idea a step further by adopting the technique of silk-screening, turning out hundreds of identical prints of Coca-Cola bottles and other familiar commodities, such as identical three-dimensional Brillo boxes. Rock and roll did something very similar—it turned out hundreds of identical songs, challenging the primacy of authorship that had dictated the course of Western artistic traditions since at least the Renaissance. Indeed, rock artists would play each other's songs with no regard whatsoever for authorship and copyright issues. Elvis recorded Carl Perkins' "Blue Suede Shoes, as did various other musical artists of the era. Nobody cared, legally or musically. It was the song that mattered, not who its composer was.

Pop art, like rock and roll, engaged the masses, not just the critics. But, as the critics asked, was it art? Will generations 200 years from now see it as art or as a snapshot of an era? The same question applies to the Rock Era. Will "Heartbreak Hotel" be played, let alone appreciated, in the year 2159? Neither the pop artists nor the rock and roll stars have ever shown any indication that they ever cared to answer the question—they did what they did because it was fun and because people loved it.

It is relevant to note that the pop artists saw the rock and film stars of the 1950s as key subjects of their canvasses. Warhol's most famous subjects, in fact, included not only commercial products, but 1950s celebrities such as Elvis Presley and Marilyn Monroe. Marilyn Monroe is especially critical to understanding the undercurrent of change that was occurring in the 1950s. Her great beauty made her a sex symbol. The magazines and newspapers were filled with stories about her love affairs and her various intrigues. But in spite of her success, Monroe had a tragic life, dying at the age of 36 from an overdose of sleeping pills—paralleling the death of Elvis

Photo 2.5: Richard Hamilton's *Just What Is It That Makes Today's Home So Different, So Appealing?* (1956)

Source: © R. Hamilton. All Rights Reserved, SODRAC (2017)

Presley. After her death, she became an icon, similar to religious icons, revered in the same way a martyr would have been revered in the past. No wonder Warhol made her a subject for his paintings, significantly alongside Elvis Presley.

Pop art also understood the growing power of advertising in society. James Rosenquist and Tom Wesselmann, for instance, used advertising images for their paintings, reflecting the materialism implied by them, replacing all other kinds of social meanings. The first work identified as pop art, *Just What Is It*

That Makes Today's Home So Different, So Appealing? by British artist Richard Hamilton—a collage of two ludicrous figures in a living room—was actually all about the vulgarity of materialism. It shows how a 1950s household looked—a warehouse of useless and discardable objects (see Photo 2.5).

HOLDEN CAULFIELD, *HAPPY DAYS*, AND *THE TRUMAN SHOW*

The first fictional portrayal of 1950s adolescence was J.D. Salinger's *The Catcher in the Rye* (1951). The main character of that novel, Holden Caulfield, was a 1950s idealist who, like Werther in the previous century, was disgusted by the hypocrisy and phoniness of the masses. So, Holden places his bets on children, desperately hoping to block them, especially his sister Phoebe, from growing up (at least metaphorically) and becoming just as phony and dreary as everyone else.

Holden's portraits of fellow adolescents are penetrating character profiles of 1950s teens. First, there is Robert Ackley, Holden's dorm mate at school, whose filthy habits and unseemly appearance repel him:

> He was one of the very, very tall, round-shouldered guys—he was about six four—with lousy teeth. The whole time he roomed next to me, I never even once saw him brush his teeth. They always looked mossy and awful, and he damn near made you sick if you saw him in the dining room with his mouth full of mashed potatoes and peas or something. Besides that, he had a lot of pimples. Not just on his forehead or his chin, like most guys, but all over his whole face. And not only that, he had a terrible personality.[24]

Then there is Ward Stradlater, an alpha male who exudes vanity and machismo:

He always looked good when he was finished fixing himself up, but he was a secret slob anyway, if you knew him the way I did. The reason he fixed himself up to look good was because he was madly in love with himself. He thought he was the handsomest guy in the Western hemisphere.[25]

Did Holden represent the inner struggles of young people of the 1950s? Or was he Salinger's spokesman who condemned the modern world as shallow and pretentious? The novel became a classic almost the instant it was published. It captured the spirit of 1950s in the same way that *The Great Gatsby* captured the ethos of the 1920s.

The iconic American ABC sitcom *Happy Days* (1974–1984) presents a diametrically opposed portrait of the 1950s, portraying that era as an idealized one. The narrative revolved around 1950s teenagers and their relations with parents, school, and society while they dealt with problems of maturity, romance, and an uncertain future on every episode. Its success was attributed to its nostalgic depiction of a simpler era in American history when social and gender roles, as well as traditional values, were clear-cut and largely accepted as basic. But there is also a parodic subtext throughout the sitcom. The characters are caricatures, talking the talk of the 1950s, but seeming to be strangely out of place and out of time.

The setting was Milwaukee—middle America—and the "hang out" was a diner, where a jukebox played rock and roll and the teenagers ate fast food and drank milkshakes.

The sitcom was evidence that youth culture leaves its mark, as it morphs into general adult pop culture, given that the sitcom appealed mainly to the adults of the 1970s who were teenagers in the 1950s. The makers and initial adopters of popular trends have tended to be young people since the Roaring Twenties. Although the older generations initially saw these trends as immoral or vulgar, they eventually caught on with them as well,

Photo 2.6: Henry Winkler and Ron Howard from *Happy Days* (1974)

Source: Image courtesy of ABC Television / Wikimedia Commons

gaining great appeal and entertainment value over time. This seems to be a pattern within modern-day culture—trends enacted and performed by young people eventually make their way into the mainstream culture.

Perhaps the main reason for this transference is, of course, that young people become old, holding on to the trends of their youth as they age. Trends that were once imbued with significance become, over time, elements of cultural nostalgia. To this day, there is a constant dynamic between trends that start in the youth domain and more general forms of culture in modern society. This cycle is tied to the requirements of the marketplace. In the history of modern societies, youth, social change, and the business world have always formed an implicit nexus.

Another facet to the 1950s version of youth culture was the emerging power of television to influence people directly and even construct models of reality. This is a main subtext of *The Truman Show* (1998). Directed by Peter Weir and written by Andrew Niccol, the film features a modern-day "Everyman," Truman Burbank, who is the unsuspecting star of his very own reality television show. Truman is the first baby to be legally adopted by a corporation, which films every moment of his life for television audiences to enjoy. He is seen going about his life in the largest studio ever constructed, a world within a world, without knowing that he is in it. Five thousand cameras, all controlled from a room at the top of the domed studio, follow and record his every action. Truman's friends, family, and wife are carefully selected actors. The show becomes extremely popular, with revenues equivalent to the gross national product of a country, generated by product placement. Eventually, Truman learns the truth about his simulated life, despite attempts to conceal it from him. He steps through the door of the set back into real life, leaving viewers in a quandary as to what to do and looking for something similar to entertain them on TV.

The world manufactured for Truman is a hybrid of both the old and the new, blending the society of the 1950s with the technology of the late 1990s. The idea of recreating the feel of the 1950s was to evoke the false optimism and hope of the era, exposing it as a nightmare. The citizens of Truman's world are polite and friendly, biking cheerfully to work and taking strolls down tree-lined boulevards. The setting is nostalgic. However, its integration with new technologies is a jarring one, conveying the sense that something is amiss. Truman drives a recent car model, uses an ATM card, and works on a computer. Viewers watch him bathe, sleep, and go through the motions of everyday life. Television has eliminated the difference between fiction and reality and further ensconced consumerism as a marketplace religion. Companies fight each other to have

Truman use their particular brand of coffee, eat their particular brand of chicken, and so on. Viewers can flip through *The Truman Show* catalogue and place an order, since everything on the show, from the wardrobes to the furniture, is for sale. When Truman and his wife discuss a new kitchen product, their conversation sounds like a commercial. The underlying satire of materialist society was transparent.

The Truman Show implies that contemporary people can no longer distinguish, or want to distinguish, between reality and fantasy. It is a perfect exemplification of the concept of the *simulacrum*, put forward by French philosopher Jean Baudrillard, whereby the borderline between representation and reality has vanished, turning real life into simulation and vice versa simulated life into real life.[26] The world of the 1950s is, clearly, a key one for understanding how the simulacrum came into being. *Happy Days* and *The Truman Show* provide different portraits of that same era, allowing us to see its contrasts. The essence of that era came out in rock and roll music. It changed society much more than we realize today. It did not last long, as discussed above, because the music was tamed by social taste managers to appeal to larger audiences. The rebellion had come to an end as the decade of the 1950s did.

EPILOGUE

The Rock Era ended on February 3, 1959. That was the day when three icons of the era, Buddy Holly, Richie Valens, and the Big Bopper (J.P. Richardson) died in a plane crash near Clear Lake, Iowa. Singer-songwriter Don McLean referred to that tragic event as "the day the music died," in his 1971 song "American Pie." The 1950s had come to an end—not because of a Great Depression or another World War, but simply because the music had nothing left to say to anyone. It simply died.

But why did the fade-out occur? Rock and roll lost its original *raison d'être*—rebellion against artificial social taboos, racism, and sexism. The Beat writers expressed the rebellion through their original, anti-traditional styles of writing. The pop artists rebelled against the pretentiousness of art movements that were intended primarily for the cognoscenti. The rebellion on all three fronts was largely successful. The world has, indeed, never been the same since rock and roll, Beat literature, and pop art. There is no turning back the clock. Of course, the music hardly reached sublime heights of classical music or even jazz for that matter. But it was music that *mattered*. Elvis, James Dean, and Marlon Brando, among many others, were American rebels. In their personae they communicated an intense, brooding discontent with the world. This is why, after their deaths, they became icons not only in America but also in many other parts of the world.

In an interesting work on the music of the late Buddy Holly, culture critic Fred Kaplan traces the first stirrings of the counterculture movement to the 1959 plane crash.[27] That event did indeed bring the Rock Era to an end and put the world on hold until 1964 and the arrival of a new and politically powerful rebellion. An eerie silence ensued among young people right after the crash. Something in the world had indeed changed— the baby boomers had become suddenly older and more mature, and the music of the moment no longer had meaning. Change was just around the corner.

The *Life Magazine* March 11, 2002, issue—*Rock & Roll at 50*—bears out that 1950s rock and roll had become a matter of nostalgia at the turn of the millennium. In its survey of the top 10 rock stars of all time, Elvis Presley tops the list. It is unlikely that the same list would be valid today. Rock icons resonate mainly with the generation that knew them as performers.

The 1950s also left its mark on the marketplace. Since then, teenagers have been seen as the tastemakers by the culture industries. They have shaped trends in every corner of society, from music and movies to fashion and technology. Adolescence has been good for business, because the only constant within it is inconstancy. It is no exaggeration to say that the entire economic system in which we live seems to have become completely dependent upon ensuring an incessant craving for anything new—new music, new fashion, new everything. French culture critic Roland Barthes called this artificial desire "neomania," a disease of the soul, rather than of the mind.[28] However, as Bob Dylan so aptly put it in one of his songs, the times were "a-changing" after the day the music died. A revolution, called the counterculture movement, was fomenting. The "day the music died" in the 1950s may have become the day adolescence died, at least in the way it was portrayed in *Happy Days*.

CHAPTER 3

Revolution: The Counterculture Era

It's pretty clear now that what looked like it might have been some kind of counterculture is, in reality, just the plain old chaos of undifferentiated weirdness.

—*Jerry Garcia (1942–1995)*

PROLOGUE

"His hair has the long Jesus Christ look. He is wearing the costume clothes. But most of all, he now has a very tolerant and therefore withering attitude toward all those who are still struggling in the old activist political ways ... while he, with the help of psychedelic chemicals, is exploring the infinite regions of human consciousness."[1] These words were written by American author Tom Wolfe. They paint a rather perceptive portrait of the figure of the counterculture revolutionary—an adolescent with long hair and beads, who rejects conventional values and takes hallucinogenic drugs as a means towards self-discovery.

The counterculture movement of the 1960s was, some would say, the "greatest" youth culture movement ever. Its aim was, essentially, to start a revolution against the materialistic worldview of capitalism and the social inequalities capitalism espoused. The counterculture youth literally wanted to change the world—hence go against the culture, which is the meaning of the term *counterculture*. The Beatles encapsulated this goal in their 1968 hit song, "Revolution" with the lyrics "You say you want a revolution/Well, you know/We all want to change the world." The revolution started around 1964 and ended in 1969 at the historically iconic Woodstock festival. Although short-lived, its impact on society is still being felt to this day. Indeed, in an age of political and social uncertainty, politicians from the hippie era, such as Bernie Sanders (from Vermont), have gained a huge following of young people who relate to the revolutionary verve that harkens back to the Counterculture Era. Counterculture bands, too, such as the Doors and the Velvet Underground, are finding new devoted audiences.

Counterculture youths no longer saw music as a source of fun and rebellion against parents, but rather as a powerful voice of protest against what they called "the establishment." Music had become more sophisticated in its style and lyrics. It cast a spotlight directly on the creativity of the young artists of the era. Rock and roll was still the main genre, but it had evolved considerably, developing many new subgenres, from folk rock to jazz and psychedelic rock.

As the musical diversity implied, young people no longer saw themselves as a singular lifestyle community, as they did in the 1950s. They were unified, however, at another level—by an inherent revolutionary attitude towards society. Still, the variance in approach to the revolution was played out in distinctive groups and subcultures, each with its own allegiance to a particular type of music and the ideology on which it was based. While the Rock Era had developed a "split personality" by the end (Chapter 2), the same type of poetic licence can be used to characterize the Counterculture Era as having "multiple personalities" within the same revolutionary body. So, despite the eclecticism and diversification, the movement showed that music, as in the 1920s and 1950s, was still the key to understanding shifts in youth culture and what the movement entailed vis-à-vis the larger society. Moreover, to the adult world, the new movement was still perceived as a monolithic one, at least at first. Only by the end of the 1960s did society become aware of the "helter skelter" nature of the movement, as the Beatles put it in their emblematic 1968 song.

The counterculture music deepened the meaning of rock and roll. It dealt with sex, death, love, fear, rebellion against society, the search for self-knowledge, engagement with the dark side of the psyche, and various socio-political themes. It soon became obvious to one and all that the Counterculture Era was not just another lifestyle movement; it was a truly revolutionary one, characterized by drugs, randomness in living (helter skelter), and a rejection of the traditional goals of America, often called the American Dream, which amounted to the achievement of material well-being through hard work. The dream was based on the Protestant ethic, as sociologist Max Weber termed it at the turn of the twentieth century.[2] Weber argued that the religious ideologies of groups such as the Calvinists (who believed in a rigid religious lifestyle based on denial of earthly pleasures) created modern-day corporate capitalism, which sees profit as an end in itself, pursuing it as if it were the equivalent of religious virtue. Weber went on to argue that this broke down the traditional economic system based on ownership by families, paving the way for modern corporate capitalism. Once the latter had emerged, the original Protestant values were no longer required, as the "ethic" on which they were based took on a new capitalist life of its own.

The counterculture youths attacked this ethic from the outset at the same time that they sought to inject a new form of spiritualism into their world based on Eastern philosophies and techniques, such as meditation. They became "wanderers" of mind and spirit, recalling the wanderer youth stories of the past, where youth is portrayed as a period of wantonness and foolishness, but also idealism. The story of the Buddha is among the most emblematic of these.

The Buddha (Siddhartha Gautama) left home as a young man, leaving behind family and wealth, in search of self-knowledge, having become restless and filled with sadness and sorrow. During his wanderings, he encountered an aged man, a sick man, and a corpse. From these encounters he realized that suffering was an inescapable part of life, whereupon he determined to forsake wealth and power in the quest for truth—in the quest for answering the question of why life exists in the first place.

It is little wonder that one of the novels admired by counterculture youths was Hermann Hesse's *Siddhartha*, which was all about the spiritual journey. The novel was actually published in 1922, but it was not until the 1960s that it became a cult phenomenon, constituting a metaphor for the times. In the novel, the character Siddhartha is shown at first as being spiritually dissatisfied, believing that the elders in his community had nothing more to teach him. He decides to join the Samanas, a group of wandering ascetics. Siddhartha and his best friend, Govinda, who accompanies him on his journey, spend three years learning how to withstand pain and hunger in an effort to transcend the body's limitations. Although the two friends learn a lot from this way of life, they are still dissatisfied and decide to go and meet the Buddha. Govinda is impressed and chooses to join the Buddha's community, but Siddhartha decides to continue on his quest, travelling to a nearby town where he is mesmerized by the beauty of the courtesan Kamala. He offers himself to her, but she rebuffs him, saying that she is interested only in someone who is rich. Siddhartha begins working and eventually becomes Kamala's lover. Over time, however, he becomes restless once again, and one morning he simply walks away from his cozy life. After considering suicide, he encounters a ferryman and asks to become his apprentice. The ferryman accepts Siddhartha as his companion. The river becomes Siddhartha's spiritual guide through which he grows wiser. Only then does he achieve enlightenment, ferrying people across the river, having found simple meaning in life.

As mentioned, the counterculture movement was greatly attracted by Eastern philosophy and religion, especially Buddhism. Indeed, the counterculture movement incorporated many of elements of Buddhism into its lifestyle and the music. Hesse's novel became a kind of implicit sacred text for the spiritual quest of the movement.

The theme of wandering is a Jungian archetype—an unconscious pattern in the psyche that is expressed in symbolic and narrative forms.[3] The wanderer archetype is found in all kinds of cultural narratives, from ancient myths to modern day movies. Self-knowledge comes from the journey, imaginary or real. The counterculture youth took that journey as well; but it occurred primarily through drugs. In fact, they called it a *trip*, in reference to the altered state of consciousness induced by the consumption of psychedelic drugs—a trip outside the body. A common slogan for the period was, actually, "sex, drugs, and rock and roll," alluding to the view of sexual relations as necessarily "open," of drugs as the path to self-knowledge, and rock and roll as the aesthetic pulse guiding the journey.

In the 1950s, rebellion was more imaginary than it was real, symbolized by movies such as *Rebel without a Cause*. In the Counterculture Era, the rebellion became spiritually, politically, philosophically, and aesthetically real, as the new generation of teenagers became "rebels with a cause," openly questioning the values of the society in which they were reared as never before. Called colloquially *hippies*, they denounced the adult establishment publicly, seeking inspiration from diverse sources, such as folk and mystical traditions. They used music to spearhead the clamour for social change. The open-air rock concert became a true tribal ritual. Drugs were consumed to induce or heighten the musical and group-bonding experience of the whole event. Sexual activities were practised openly, in front of television cameras, in blatant defiance of adult moralism. The new rock and roll was ambitious in many ways. Indeed, musicians no longer referred to the music as *rock and roll*, but just *rock*, differentiating themselves from the 1950s artists. It was no longer just music for dancing. In fact, there is no such thing as "counterculture dance music." This would have been a true oxymoron. The artistic voices included performers and bands such as Bob Dylan, Joan Baez, Joe Cocker, Van Morrison, Simon & Garfunkel, the Mamas & the Papas, the Band, the Rolling Stones, Credence Clearwater Revival, the Doors, Jimi Hendrix, the Byrds, Procol Harum, Pink Floyd, and, of course, the Beatles. The lyrics denounced apathy, warmongering, racism, gender inequality, stereotyping, and other social ills. They also praised spirituality over materialism.

By the end of the 1960s, rock operas, such as *Tommy* (1969) by the Who, were being considered as serious works by mainstream music critics. The Counterculture Era had thus produced a veritable revolution in both society and musical art. It was obvious that the transformation that youth culture had undergone in little more than a decade was a radical one indeed.

THE BEATLES

The influence of the British rock group the Beatles on the emergence and entrenchment of counterculture rock, and indeed the whole counterculture movement, cannot be underestimated. Elvis Presley was the regal figurehead of the teenage world in the 1950s; the Beatles took his throne in the 1960s. Coming out of the working-class slums of Liverpool, England, the band—consisting of Paul McCartney, John Lennon, George Harrison, and Ringo Starr—became a sensation by 1964. Their long hair and their dress style (which included boots) became the general model of early counterculture fashion, although from this very code only the penchant for long hair remained as the movement progressed. "Beatlemania" was as intense as "Elvismania" had been a decade earlier. With truly remarkable albums such as *Rubber Soul* (1965) and *Sgt. Pepper's Lonely Hearts Club Band* (1967), the Beatles were revolutionizing youth culture from within, imbuing it with a much more mature aesthetic and philosophical character.

In 1964, the Beatles toured the United States and created excitement everywhere they performed. It was obvious that the 1950s Rock Era was over and that a new one had come forward spearheaded by the British group. The band made a famous television appearance on *The Ed Sullivan Show* on February 9, 1964. Like it did for Elvis a decade earlier, that variety show established the Beatles as the leaders of a new and pulsating youth culture.

Most counterculture scholars maintain that the Beatles' 1967 album *Sgt. Pepper's Lonely Hearts Club Band* was the one that signalled a paradigm shift in youth culture, although this was arguably prefigured in their marvelous 1965 album *Rubber Soul*. The music on both albums was truly original for the times.

Photo 3.1: The Early Beatles

Source: Pictorial Press Ltd / Alamy Stock Photo

Sgt. Pepper's was also the first concept album of rock and roll. Previously, an album would contain a collection of songs by an artist, with no thematic link among the set. But *Sgt. Pepper's* changed all that, once and for all. Although concept albums go back to the 1930s, for rock and roll this was a veritable innovation.

The cover was itself revolutionary. It was designed by two pop artists, Peter Blake and Jann Haworth, from a sketch by McCartney. It was a collage in the classic pop art style, featuring the band standing behind a drum skin. In front is an arrangement of flowers spelling out the name "Beatles." The group members are dressed in glowing multi-colored military-style uniforms. After the release of the album, this became a kind of dress code, spreading broadly among counterculture youths. We can also see wax sculptures of the band members, along with photographs depicting a diversity of famous people, from actors and sports figures to scientists, religious and political leaders, and great writers. This is truly a work of pop art, eliminating the boundaries between high and low culture (see Photo 3.2).

The album was a masterpiece. In its lyrics and overall musical structure, it constituted a musical essay on the modern world, raising many questions about modern life, and life in general, bringing us all on a journey, or more accurately, on a drugless "trip." One of the songs, "Lucy in the Sky with Diamonds," is arguably about LSD itself (since the title is constructed with the first letters of the drug) and its role in the counterculture movement. As the well-known song from the 1968 musical *Hair* put it, the album signalled the dawning of a new age—an "Age of Aquarius," which astrologically signifies newness and non-conformity. Most of the counterculture albums that followed also featured cover art that was, itself, aesthetically and thematically important. The focus shifted away from the rock celebrity to the content of the music. The world of youth-based music has never been the same since.

Photo 3.2: Cover for *Sgt. Pepper's Lonely Hearts Club Band*

Source: Pictorial Press Ltd / Alamy Stock Photo

THE COUNTERCULTURE ERA

The Age of Aquarius was a synonym for the Counterculture Era. Such an age was thought to stress the values of love, brotherhood, integrity, and unity, rather than hate and warmongering. This implied that the pre-existing order of governments, corporations, and traditional institutions must be taken down. In their place, the dawning of heightened consciousness would come over everyone and peace and harmony would rule the world.

This, in essence, was the hippie philosophy. It was idealism, pure and simple, but idealism is crucial for building or rebuilding societies. The movement was young people's particular take on creating utopia (as they saw it).

The Age of Aquarius did not crystallize at the start of the movement; it came about after the release of *Sgt. Pepper's Lonely Hearts Club Band.* It then came to a head in Berkeley, San Francisco, and New York, spearheaded by the hippies with their long hair, bell-bottom jeans, and colourful shirts, often in imitation of the dress of the Beatles on the album's cover. The dawning of the new consciousness was triggered by music, drugs, open sexuality, and meditation. Unlike the sock hops of the previous era, the rock concert was experienced as a momentous enlightening event, not a reason for having fun. One rock concert in particular has come to symbolize the whole counterculture movement, taking place just as the movement was petering out. It has gained mythic status as a "final battle" scene of the counterculture revolution. That concert was the one held near Woodstock in upstate New York in 1969 on fields owned by a farmer. Many of the great counterculture musicians were there. Despite the fact that the festival had attracted over 300,000 rock fans over three days, one could sense that the end was coming, that the revolution was fading. So, in the end, the counterculture revolution really lasted three years—1967 (after the release of *Sgt. Pepper's*), 1968, and 1969 (with the Woodstock concert). But they were intense, controversial, and dramatic years nonetheless. During those years, it was becoming increasingly obvious that youth culture was no longer simply an optional and temporary culture for young people, as in the 1920s and 1950s; it had itself developed into a revolutionary ideological paradigm that was permanently changing the mindset and ethos of modern society.

Elvis culture was, as discussed, all about a symbolic rebellion against anything that smacked of adulthood. The elders of the era could not figure out why the teenagers were rebelling, with food on the table and advanced schooling available to whoever could afford it. The silent rebellion, nevertheless, brought about a critical shift in society, with young people no longer seen as "developing adults," but as makers of culture and art. Still, the Rock Era did not threaten the establishment overtly. Indeed, youth, business, and the media formed an intrinsic partnership that echoed back to the type of partnership established in the Roaring Twenties. At first, the counterculture movement aimed to dismantle this partnership, although it eventually succumbed to it. But for those three critical years, 1967, 1968, and 1969, the rebellion was becoming truly subversive, rather than just symbolically transgressive. The early counterculture artists and bands did not pose a menace; they were seen simply as descendants of their Rock Era counterparts. The Beatles and the Rolling Stones, for instance, at first simply took the music of the previous era and gave it a new "oomph." The early counterculture music was, in fact, influenced by the music of Chuck Berry, Buddy Holly, and the Everly Brothers. But this was only a preface to what was to come, during a time when sweeping social change was percolating, brought about by the assassination of John F. Kennedy and the expansion of the Vietnam War. There is little doubt that the killing of Kennedy, a young and idealistic president, was felt to have been a *coup d'état* by the extreme political right of America. A desire to restore the idealism of the dead president was truly fomenting below the veneer. By 1967, the percolation temperature had reached a boiling point, with public protests, sit-ins of all kinds, and public demonstrations of defiance popping up everywhere.

The climax came in 1968, the year in which the revolution truly took to the streets everywhere, as rebellions against the social elites, and especially the "military-industrial" complex of the capitalist world, as the hippies called it, occurred everywhere, leading often to tragedies, such as the Kent State University shootings a few years later in May of 1970, when

Photo 3.3: Iconic Photo of the Kent State Massacre

Source: John Filo / Premium Archive / Getty Images

soldiers were dispatched to the campus to remove protestors. The soldiers fired shots into the crowd, killing four students and wounding nine others. The tragedy of the moment was captured by an iconic photo that has come to symbolize the calamitous and catastrophic events that the era engendered (see Photo 3.3).

Wildcat strikes, escalating guerrilla warfare, and disruptions of governments and businesses had started posing a serious threat to capitalism itself. The civil rights movement also took a military turn with the founding of the Black Panthers, which espoused violence to support the clamour for change. Opposition to war also became a worldwide phenomenon. Clearly, the world was in a revolutionary mood, thanks in no small part to the counterculture movement.

Spearheading the revolution was the music and the diverse lifestyles associated with it, including those based on hallucinogenic drugs. The hippies were no longer pegged as spoiled brats, as were the 1950s teens; they were perceived as "radicals" and part of a subversive political movement that aimed to bring about fundamental change to society and even its overthrow. Actually, the hippies themselves were ineffectual in directly bringing about change. But they set the stage for the media and social activists to demand change; and change they got. Sexual equality laws, anti-discrimination legislation, and even the end of the Vietnam War can be traced ultimately to these "radicals."

Many politicians and business leaders decried the hippie movement as destructive of traditional mores. Even those who favoured it at the time had to acknowledge that, overall, it tended to veer off into nihilism and even violence, instilling in young people a worldview that challenged the very puritanical and capitalist foundations of American society and its constituent institutions, from the traditional family to religion. In a phrase, being a hippie meant being someone intent on overthrowing capitalism. The young hippies were not alone, of course. Some of the "older hippies," who were mainly in academia, formed the political movement known as the New Left together with their younger counterparts, opposing many of the academic traditions of the past. It was "New" in relation to the "Old Left" guided by Marxist ideas. The New Left movement demanded sweeping and fundamental changes to the capitalist "bottom-line" ethic. They openly critiqued major institutions, public and private, for hypocritically claiming to support democratic principles but failing to put an end to such injustices as sexism, poverty, racial discrimination, and class distinctions.

Members of the New Left favoured civil disobedience, which often led to bloody clashes with the authorities. This appealed especially to the hippies, whose peace demonstrations demanded a general reformation of American society. Several radical student organizations appeared, including the Students for a Democratic Society (SDS) and the Free Speech

Photo 3.4: Vietnam War Protestors (1967)

Source: Photo by Frank Wolfe, Lyndon B. Johnson Library, courtesy of Wikimedia Commons

Movement. These groups considered even the university as an accomplice of the war machine and as an institution that continued to support racism.

But the real menace to the establishment was the music. The new styles included not only the influential experiments of the Beatles but also San Francisco psychedelic rock, the hard rock of Jimi Hendrix and Eric Clapton, jazz rock, and folk rock, among others. Soul music, the successor to rhythm and blues, emerged with a wide range of styles of its own, including the gospel-based songs of Aretha Franklin, the funk techniques of James Brown, and the soulful crooning of Marvin Gaye. But perhaps no one epitomized the new brash revolutionary attitude more than the Rolling Stones. The lead singer, Mick Jagger, did not "sing" his songs; he screamed them with an angry voice. His 1965 song, "Satisfaction," shook the world to its foundations. It was abrasive, threatening, yet appealing. It expressed the emerging counterculture attitude perfectly. Mick could not get any satisfaction, as he put it, no matter how much he tried. The frustration is tangible in both his screeching voice and the repeating lyrics of the song. And the source of the frustration is the hypocrisy and superficiality of society. "The man on the radio," for example, gives Mick nothing but "useless information," and the man on TV does nothing more than tell him "how white his shorts can be." In that one song, all of society is condemned and chastised. It called out desperately, screechingly, for a change.

THE HIPPIES

It is relevant to note that the word *hippie* is a derivative of *hip*, which, as discussed in the previous chapter, had been around for quite a number of years, alongside *hipster*, the term used in reference to the Beat writers of the early 1950s (as we saw). It was a short step from hipster culture to the hippie one, which came to national attention in January of 1967, in San Francisco's

Golden Gate Park, when 20,000 hippies held the first "Human Be-In," as a sign of protest against the materialism and bellicosity of American society. The summer of that year came to be known as the "Summer of Love," marking the full arrival of hippie culture on the scene.

As social scientist John Howard put it at the height of the counterculture movement, the hippies "posed a fairly well thought-out alternative to conventional society and, importantly, for the notion of a counter-culture, there was some sense that this alternative mode of living would induce change in the rest of society."[4] Howard went on to identify four types of hippies, all of whom, in their own way, typified a stand against some element of the establishment. First, there were the "visionaries," who were the utopians in the movement, energetically devising alternatives to the existing social institutions through music, actions, and manifestos. Then there were the "freaks" and "heads," who were drug-using hippies who relished the experience of altered states of awareness, seeing them as a path to social reform (presumably if everyone else used them regularly as well); they also delved into the occult and Eastern philosophies and religions. The "plastic hippies" were really not hippies at all but young people who dressed like them as a matter of fashion. Finally, there were the "midnight hippies," who were older people sympathetic to the reforms and bohemian values of the hippies but who retained their basic "non-hippie" lifestyle.[5]

Did this concoction of seemingly weird individuals really change America and the world? It did; not only because of the protests in the streets, but especially because of the music. It was both harmonic and melodic, but also raucous when the content required it. Moral panic grabbed the nation at first. What Plato had feared most in his own time about music had seemingly come about in the hippie world of the 1960s. As he astutely pointed out, "For the introduction of a new kind of music must be shunned as imperiling the whole state; since styles of music are never disturbed without affecting the most important political institutions."[6] Counterculture rock certainly seemed to imperil the modern political institutions.[7]

Was the hippie movement unique in history? It was not. As Ken Goffman has argued, countercultures have been around since time immemorial—operating, at times, below the social radar and, at others, fuelling subversive energy that ends up changing the world. The need for change is a condition of humanity, and the occasional emergence of a counterculture is one of its manifestations. He puts it as follows:

> Counterculture blooms wherever and whenever a few members of a society choose lifestyles, artistic expressions, and ways of thinking and being that wholeheartedly embrace the ancient axiom that the only true constant is change itself. The mark of counterculture is not a particular social form or structure, but rather the evanescence of forms and structures, the dazzling rapidity and flexibility with which they appear, mutate, and morph into one another and disappear.[8]

The "forms and structures" of the hippie counterculture, to use Goffman's phraseology, were hallucinogenic drugs, psychedelic art, light shows, demonstrations in favour of peace and free love, and of course a powerful new music that called into question the mores of the social order and especially of bourgeois and consumerist culture. The subtext in the music was the need to achieve a "brotherhood of man," as John Lennon phrased it in his brilliant song "Imagine." But the music was not just about the revolution; it also expanded the structural possibilities of rock and roll. Jerry Garcia and the Grateful Dead, for example, experimented with long, improvised stretches of music called "jams." In the 1950s, songs lasted, in contrast, from two to three minutes. Some musicians even turned away from the aesthetic canons of Western musical traditions, seeking inspiration from Eastern ones instead. The Beatles introduced Ravi Shankar to the counterculture movement. He was an Indian musician who became well known throughout the world for his inspired playing of the string instrument called the sitar, which the Beatles incorporated into some of their compositions.

Some critics, however, see the counterculture movement as vastly different from the portrait described here. Nadya Zimmerman, for example, suggests that the revolution was more theatre than real.[9] But this view ignores the political upheavals ignited by the movement in 1968, as mentioned above, and the many changes that it brought about through legislation that would have likely never have been contemplated without it. Certainly, the riot at the 1968 Democratic National Convention in Chicago was hardly theatre. The counterculture youths had disrupted a key part of the political process but in so doing raised awareness about the nature of politics itself. Joseph H. Heath and Andrew P. Potter also see the movement as somewhat superficial, being perfectly compatible with the goals of a consumerist culture.[10] The movement thus unwittingly created the conditions that have led to a supercharged consumer society:

> Hippies bought VW Beetles for one primary reason—to show that they rejected mass society. The big three Detroit automakers had been the target of withering social criticism for well over a decade, accused of promoting "planned obsolescence" in their vehicles. They were chastised above all for changing their models and designs so that consumers would be forced to buy a new car every few years in order to keep up with the Joneses. The tail fin was held up by many as an object of special scorn— as both an embodiment and symbol of the wastefulness of American consumer culture. Against this backdrop,

> Volkswagen entered the US consumer market with a very
> simple pitch: Wanna show people that you're not just a cog
> in the machine? Buy our car![11]

There may be some truth to this critique. Volkswagen's success among the counterculture youths caught the attention of the business world. Corporate America began cleverly to see the wisdom of turning to young people for inspiration and even advice on how to market their products. As a result, Heath and Potter suggest implicitly, the rebellion gradually morphed into big business. The 1999 film *American Beauty* also touched upon this. The film's characters are divided into two groups: counterculture rebels and establishment conformists. The former all behave in identifiable ways: they smoke dope, are involved in human causes, and praise the beauty of nature; the latter are neurotic and sexually repressed, obsess over what others think of them, and play with handguns. Colonel Fitts, the symbolic embodiment of the establishment persona, beats his son while screaming that the boy needs order and discipline—and the good Colonel collects Nazi memorabilia as well. But was it really that way, the film asks? Was there a veritable clash of cultures in the hippie era? In effect, the film challenges the view of the hippies as idealistic youths and establishment individuals as bigoted pariahs. Even Beat poet Allen Ginsberg was quoted as saying in a 1994 *Time* magazine interview that the whole counterculture movement was, in the end, "an upper-bourgeois life-style con. A camouflage for egocentricity and commercial theatrics."[12]

Another bleak portrait of hippie culture can be painted—the inherent danger of self-appointed counterculture leaders, who ended up distorting the counterculture movement. This is the opinion of Gary Lachman, who asks in his book *Turn Off Your Mind*, "How did a decade of peace and love end in Altamont and the Manson Family bloodbath?"[13] Lachman is

referring to the Tate-LaBianca murders, which occurred in
1969. Screen actress Sharon Tate Polanski was murdered at
her Bel-Air home in Benedict Canyon early in the morning
of August 10 along with coffee heiress Abigail Folger and
her common-law husband Wojiciech Frykowski, as well as
Hollywood hair stylist Jay Sebring and delivery boy Steven Earl
Parent. Supermarket chain president Leno LaBianca and his
wife Rosemary were murdered later in the day in Los Angeles.
The murders were planned and executed by members of a hippie
cult family led by an ex-convict named Charles Manson. The
motive was Manson's personal vendetta against society. He had
brainwashed his hippie followers with drugs, sex, and pseudo-
religious platitudes, ordering them to commit the horrific murders. Together with satanic themes in the emerging hard rock
music of various counterculture bands, it seemed that the peace
and love motive of the decade was falling hopelessly into a dark
hole. The peace movement was becoming, Lachman suggests,
rather gruesome. Add to this the appearance of para-military
groups like the Symbionese Liberation Army, whose goal was
to overthrow society by military-style violence, and one can see
the logic of Lachman's argument.

All this is true, but it happened after the counterculture
movement was on the wane. The fact remains that it did indeed
raise awareness of social issues. If there is a greater degree of
gender equality, racial tolerance, and sensitivity to ecologi-
cal matters today, we can thank the counterculture movement
for it, in very great part. No wonder that the movement came
into favour with intellectuals such as Herbert Marcuse of the
Frankfurt School and psychologists such as Timothy Leary.
The movement denounced the business, military, and political
complex as the cause of all social ills. They may have been ex-
aggerating, of course. But they raised awareness, and this is, in
itself, a remarkable event.

COOPTION

Capitalism thrived despite the hippie revolution. There are many reasons for this; and it would be well beyond the scope of the present treatment to discuss them in any detail. Suffice it to say here that one of the strategies developed by the business world to counteract the revolution was, as Thomas Frank has argued, to coopt it.[14] Cooption involved extracting counter-culture themes, trends, lifestyles, and emphases and adapting them to marketplace objectives, creating a tacit and clever interplay between business and the revolution. That was not done by the hippies; it was done, despite them, by the business world. In a phrase, it was not done by them, but to them.

Aware of the peril that counterculture radicalism might bring to the bottom line, businesses joined the revolution by proxy. Cooption was (and continues to be) based on the premise that the appeal of a brand increases if it can be linked to socially significant trends and values. By the late 1960s, it had become obvious that hippie culture could be transformed into the symbolic fuel for propelling corporate identity and solidifying the marketplace. In other words, as Frank argued, capitalism had countered the counterculture by incorporating it into marketing.[15] The symbolism and lifestyle patterns of the revolution were transformed into consumerist images. This may have been more of an unwitting strategy, though, since, as Frank points out, the business world really did not understand the ethos of the hippie movement at all. As he puts it, "The curious enthusiasm of American business for the symbols, music, and slang of the counterculture marked a fascination that was much more complex than the theory of co-optation [cooption] would suggest."[16]

Counterculture clothing fashion was thus quickly converted into mainstream fashion by clothing companies such as Levi Strauss & Co.; counterculture music became mainstream, recorded by major labels; and so on and so forth. By 1969, when the hippie movement was on the verge of dissipation, the revolution became an ersatz consumerist one. Every individual, hippie or not, could feel that he or she was "part of the revolution." All the individual had to do was buy the appropriate clothing item, drink the right soft drink, and listen to the right music.

Marketers had discovered, in other words, that it was in their best interest not to fight youth insurgency or subversive symbolism but rather to embrace it outright. Their main technique was the development of an advertising style that mocked consumerism and advertising itself. It worked. Being young and rebellious came to mean having a "cool look"; being anti-establishment and subversive came to mean wearing "hip clothes." The corporate brands had indeed joined the revolution, simply by deploying images of youthful subversion to market their goods and services. *Young* and *different* became the two key words of the new advertising lexicon. Campaigns, such as Coca-Cola's "Universal Brotherhood," directly incorporated the images, rhetoric, and symbolism of the counterculture movement into their style and content. With the emblematic jingle "I'd like to teach the world to sing in perfect harmony," the Coke campaigns showed the extent to which the counterculture message had become branded. The ads typically displayed images of young people living in harmony—a basic ideal of the hippies—but drinking a Coke with the tagline, "I'd like to buy the world a Coke."

The Dodge Rebellion and Oldsmobile Youngmobile campaigns were similar, etching into the nomenclature of the car models themselves the powerful connotations of hippie rebellion and defiance. Ironically, by claiming to be a part of the social revolution, the big brands created their own revolution—a revolution in how they marketed and advertised their products. But cooption notwithstanding, the counterculture movement itself did not buy into the ruse. Right until the end, at Woodstock, they fought the bottom-line philosophy of capitalism that had become destructive of the ecology, of the arts, and of the human spirit. In a sense, the counterculture movement was a descendant of the Frankfurt School's attack of the modern capitalist world.

The School was originally located at the University of Frankfurt (1923–1933). With the rise of the Nazi party, it was relocated to Geneva, Switzerland (1933–1935), and then to New York (Columbia University, 1935–1949) before returning to the University of Frankfurt in 1949. The members of the School, including Max Horkheimer, Theodor Adorno, and Herbert Marcuse, critiqued capitalism and its manipulation of culture as if it were part of a commodity-exchange system. They were highly pessimistic about the possibility of genuine culture under modern capitalism, condemning most forms of mass culture as channels of consumerist propaganda that indoctrinated the masses and disguised genuine social inequalities. For the School, capitalist culture was vulgar, functioning primarily to pacify ordinary people. It was part of a commodity industry whereby art works, like commodities, were easily discarded since they had no lasting value. Herbert Marcuse called works of art in this system commodity forms.[17] However, Marcuse, one of the younger members of the School, came to see counterculture music as the exception. Indeed, he praised it as an anomaly, since it too fought against the commodification of art.

INFLUENCES

The counterculture movement did not emerge in a vacuum; it arose in the context of various aesthetic, philosophical, and ideological movements and events that, directly or indirectly, coalesced to produce it. One of these—nihilism—seems especially relevant.

American society has been founded on the quest for happiness, which artists and writers of the era, including the pop artists, saw as a comical, ludicrous philosophy. The words of a leading figure in the absurdist-nihilist movement, Samuel Beckett, from his play *Endgame*, brought this out as follows: "Nothing is funnier than unhappiness, I grant you that. Yes, yes, it's the most comical thing in the world."[18] In his novels and plays, Beckett focused on the wretchedness of this quest, since it leads to nothingness. There is little doubt that the hippies also saw the quest as an absurd and comical one. However, unlike the absurdists and nihilists, they aimed to imbue it with more depth, starting with a reform of capitalism and an elimination of all the social ills that it engendered. So, in retrospect it can be suggested that the hippie movement was an anti-nihilistic one, even though, like the nihilists, it detected the problems that had plagued the modern world since the arrival of mass corporate capitalism.

Beckett was a major figure in the movement known as the Theater of the Absurd, which emerged in France in the 1950s. Absurdist playwrights dramatized what they believed was the essentially meaningless nature of life. Absurdist drama is psychologically powerful. Take, as a case in point, the play *Waiting for Godot*, published in 1952 by Beckett. It is a scathing indictment of the religious-philosophical belief that there is a central meaning to life beyond human control. The play fascinated modern audiences because, like the two tramps in the play, people in the twentieth century seemed to have literally "lost faith," having become cynical about everything. Even today, the play challenges our ingrained belief that there is an inherent meaning to life, insinuating that all our meaning-making systems (philosophy, religion, etc.) are no more than illusory screens we have set up to avoid the truth—that life is an absurd moment of consciousness on its way to extinction.

Photo 3.5: Samuel Beckett

Source: Photo by Roger Pic, courtesy of Wikimedia Commons

Waiting for Godot became highly popular during the Counterculture Era across North American campuses. Perhaps its nihilistic subtext was a factor in spurring on the need to go beyond the society of the times and reform it with a new purpose other than the achievement of material happiness. The evidence for this comes from some of the lyrics of the groups of the era, such as those of Pink Floyd (a late counterculture band) and especially of the Velvet Underground, founded in 1964. It comes as little surprise that the band was managed for a brief period of time by pop artist Andy Warhol—an artist who bridged the 1950s and the 1960s. The band's provocative subject matter and nihilistic lyrics actually became the forerunner of punk and alternative styles in the 1970s. The band did not achieve great commercial success, given the avant-garde nature of their music. Their debut album, *The Velvet Underground & Nico*, was dubbed one the greatest counterculture albums ever made, and in 2003, *Rolling Stone* ranked the band as 19th on its list of the 100 greatest artists of all time. With Warhol, the band's concerts revolved around film projections in the background, and stroboscopic light shows, which forced band members to wear sunglasses on stage—all props that would come to define subsequent youth culture concerts, including those by Kiss and others. The music was a musical form of pop art, a parody of the traditional assumptions about certainty, identity, and truth.

But despite the Velvet Underground's nihilism, many youths of the era seemed paradoxically to discover meaning in the band's music—a need to bring down the status quo through transgressive, non-traditional performances and musical styles. Indeed, nihilism formed just one strand in the fabric of counterculture music. Another one was a retrieval of classicism and the poetic functions of music. The group which most exemplified this was Procol Harum, a British rock band formed in 1967—at the height of the counterculture movement. Their music was an antidote to the nihilism of the Velvet Underground—it was poetic, based on baroque and classical harmonies and hauntingly beautiful melodies. Their best known song, "A Whiter Shade of Pale" (1967), is considered a classic paean to the whole counterculture movement itself. In fact, if one asked people to choose a song that epitomized the whole counterculture movement, "A Whiter Shade of Pale" would likely be named frequently, especially by those who lived through the movement.

What, one could legitimately ask, was going on? How could political protests, para-military movements, nihilism, and musical poetics exist in tandem and in parallel? All that can be said is that the counterculture movement mirrored the

Photo 3.6: Procol Harum

Source: Poppix Media Ltd / Alamy Stock Photo

social fragmentation of society. It is a mistake to consider the counterculture movement a homogeneous one. Unlike the Flapper and Rock Eras, which were fairly unified around a common musical script, the Counterculture Era involved diverse kinds of styles and approaches, even radically so, as can be seen in the music of the Velvet Underground versus that of Procol Harum. Even the better known bands, such as the Beatles and the Rolling Stones, did not really subscribe to a singular style; rather they developed eclectic styles over time. The Counterculture Era was, in a word, fragmented or, more accurately, free-form. There was a common goal, however—the quest to change the world for the better. There was also a common type of lifestyle, based on "sex, drugs, and rock and roll," as mentioned. But gone were the fun-based sock hops and the television programs of the 1950s that catered to the adolescents of the era.

The fragmentation was also imported to television. The primary example of this was a comedy program called *Rowan & Martin's Laugh-In*, which ran on NBC from 1968 to 1973. Unlike traditional comedy programs, this one reflected the character of the fragmented times in its script. The title was a play on the hippie notion of "love-in" and was thus a parody of both hippie culture and the society from which it sprang and against which the hippies railed. Each episode consisted of a series of rapid-fire lines, gags, and sketches, disconnected thematically, thus mirroring the heterogeneity of the times—a period in history without a philosophical or religious centre, just a series of comedic skits.

One other source of influence on the Counterculture Era that is worth mentioning here was occultism.[19] Groups like the Beatles, the Rolling Stones, and other counterculture bands and artists, along with their countless followers, introduced (or more correctly reintroduced) everything from the tarot, the I Ching, astrology, Cabala, yogis, and witchcraft to J.R. Tolkein's *Lord of the Rings* to their audiences.[20] But such things have always been part and parcel of carnival fare, where fortune tellers and tarot card readers entertained people alongside carnival freaks. The need to "escape the prison house of the flesh," as Lachman put it, has often been satisfied by occult practices and traditions.[21] This influence became even more pronounced in subsequent youth cultures. Suffice it to say here that occultist ideas surfaced in the Counterculture Era as yet another means to combat the endemic materialism of the times. In a way, the era aimed to create a new mythological foundation for America. The mythology of the American Dream had run its course. A new one was needed.

EPILOGUE

In 1969, a horrific event occurred that changed everything, becoming a factor that brought down the hippie movement virtually overnight. The event was the Charles Manson murders, discussed briefly above. The murders made headlines. What made them shocking was that they were planned and executed by members of a hippie cult family, led by Manson, for no other reason than to carry out Manson's personal whims, as a white supremacist, of bringing about a racial war which he would lead. Manson wanted to bring about "helter skelter," in reference to the famous Beatle song. According to Brooks Poston, a member of the cult, Manson told the group on New Year's Eve 1968, "Are you hep to what the Beatles are saying? Helter Skelter is coming down. The Beatles are telling it like it is."[22] The phrase *helter skelter* was splattered on the refrigerator at the LaBianca home.

By the early 1970s, the counterculture movement had virtually disappeared. In addition to the jarring effects of the

Tate-LaBianca murders, the hippies had, simply, become less inclined to revolt, as they started to have children of their own. New musical trends emerged, as did new youth lifestyles. Ironically, as their own children grew into adolescence, the ex-hippies became terrified. The trend that worried them the most was so-called punk music, which emerged in the mid-1970s. Alienating themselves visibly from mainstream culture, the punks were deliberately violent and confrontational, and they rejected the very revolution that their parents had espoused. Unlike the counterculture bands that engaged audiences in a "love-in" fashion, the punks spat on their audiences, mutilated themselves with knives, damaged the props on stage and in the hall, shouted, burped, urinated, and bellowed at will to a basic rhythmic pulsating beat, inciting their fans to follow suit. The fashion trends they introduced—chains, dog collars, army boots, and hairstyles, ranging from shaved heads to the wild-looking "Mohawk" hairdos of every colour imaginable—communicated degradation, mockery, social caricature, and insubordination at once. The punks were anti-bourgeois and anti-capitalist in ways that, ironically, their hippie parents found offensive. The punks espoused many of the same goals of the hippies, but their approach was vastly different. In some ways, they wanted to retrieve the minimalist simplicity of Rock Era music.

The Woodstock festival was the final chapter of the hippie era, although elements of the movement extended into the early 1970s, and some today have revived some of the hippie ideals, politically and socially. Interestingly, Woodstock was exactly a decade after the 1959 plane crash that brought the Elvis era to an end. That was called "the day the music died"; the Woodstock event can be called, analogously, "the day the revolution died."

Photo 3.7: Woodstock

Source: United Archives GmbH / Alamy Stock Photo

The energy and verve of the movement had faded through the aging process. Many of the people who attended Woodstock were much older than those who had attended the open air concerts of the previous years. There seems to be an unconscious psychic law of regression that eventually kicks into youth movements, whereby after Woodstock the hippies simply sought to settle down into more traditional settings, with their own families and jobs. Moreover, there was little left to demonstrate against, as most of the objectives of the movement were met or being met. The Vietnam War (a major reason for hippie protest) had come to an end; effective social changes brought about by the movement itself were translated into laws. The fact that there is a movement afoot today to go back in time and recapture the American Dream is truly an anomaly.

The hippie revolution instilled in America a sense that things had to change. As typically happens in mass movements, there were bound to be ups and downs. Indeed, after the end of the hippie era, in 1972, Americans re-elected Richard Nixon with one of the biggest majorities in American history—a veritable setback (despite Watergate shortly thereafter) for the deeper structural changes the hippies wanted to bring about to society. And the election of Donald Trump as president in 2016 stands in dark contrast to the hippie goals. The establishment seemed to have made a noisy and bombastic comeback. But then every society spins in historical cycles. And perhaps there is another counterculture movement fomenting in the background.

So, it is true, in the end, to say that the counterculture movement did not bring down the capitalist economic and political system based on the Protestant ethic. Indeed, corporate America is more powerful now than it was before the 1960s, the United States is still fighting wars around the world, most people still live in nuclear families (not free-love communes), drugs are still largely illegal, and so on and so forth. But today, we are all certainly more aware of what is going on and much more inclined to evaluate it critically. In the past, this would have been the domain of intellectuals. It is now the domain of virtually everyone.

Some older hippies continued to live together in small groups, sharing possessions, refusing to be tied down to a fixed job or home. They wandered from place to place seeking part-time work and temporary shelter, forming communes. Some begged for spare change and lived in the streets or camped in parks or other public lands. In time, even these hippies realized that they could not go on living in this way and that it was not possible to reform society by "dropping out" of it. The Beatles said it best with their 1968 hit "Revolution," warning hippies that if they wanted to change the world by talking about destruction then they, the Beatles, wanted out of the movement.

CHAPTER 4

Mutation: The Post-Counterculture Era

I've only been in love with a beer bottle and a mirror.

—*Sid Vicious (1957–1979)*

PROLOGUE

The term *mutation* refers, in science, to the changing structure of a physical entity, such as a gene, resulting in a variant form that may be passed on to subsequent generations, caused by the deletion, insertion, or rearrangement of larger sections of genes or chromosomes. The same term is a perfect one, as a metaphor, for characterizing virtually all youth cultures after the counterculture one, with (perhaps) the exception of the hip-hop one that flourished from the late 1980s to the early 2000s. Some would say that, after the hippie era, there never really did emerge any veritable youth culture aiming to revolutionize the world. The revolution ended at Woodstock. The movements that followed were mutations of various sorts—they carried the same genetic tendencies of the counterculture movement but in new and often unrecognizable re-combinations. Perhaps the world had changed so drastically by the 1970s that rebellions on the part of adolescents were no longer needed; or maybe the experiment itself of an independent youth culture had started to wane and become largely irrelevant.

In virtually every other movement that followed the counterculture one, there was either a linkage of various sorts with it or else a complete structural disconnection from it. In most of them, however, the premise that the music must be more than just fun (with some exceptions as we shall see) became a deeply entrenched one—the rebellion without a cause was definitely over. Whether the movement was punk or grunge or something else, there were always ideological strains within it that were acquired "genetically" from the counterculture—the music was seen as having to revolve thematically around social critique, transgression of the status quo, or around other hippie-suggestive ideals. The post-counterculture era lasted throughout the 1970s and 1980s, when hip-hop became prominent, emerging as an unexpectedly different and effective form of musical-ideological protest (as we shall see). The whole post-counterculture era can also be called the Electronic Era because the musicians started moving towards the use of electronic platforms and devices more and more. This resulted in the utilization of new equipment for the production and delivery of the music. The self-styled indie music movement of today traces its roots to this era which some characterize as the "basement music" era, given the new electronic devices that became available, which literally turned a musician's basement into a recording studio. It also resulted in a merger between television and youth musical trends with the establishment of MTV in 1981. MTV showed, in retrospect, what the mutation was all about, with its pastiche of music videos, young video jockeys who epitomized in their appearance and slang a particular trend that was in vogue at any given moment, irreverent commentary and innovative programs, promotion of new music and trends, and news and documentaries about bands and performers. One could literally see the kaleidoscopic collage of trends as they came and went, rarely coagulating into a coherent singular radical movement like the counterculture one. The clout of MTV among young people was evidenced by the fact that in 1992 both presidential candidate Bill Clinton and his running mate Al Gore appeared separately on two MTV programs in an effort to reach young voters. Today, a different medium—the Internet—is its replacement (a theme that will be broached in the final chapter).

All this does not mean that the disparate movements in the Electronic Era did not have an impact on society. They did; but not in the radical way that the Counterculture Era did. The reason may well be the heterogeneity of the movements themselves, inhibiting the possibility of cohesion and singularity of purpose. By the end of the era, youth culture, as a homogeneous entity, was clearly on the verge of demise—a demise that was put off for a few decades by various events, as we shall see; but it could not be avoided.

What did not change in this era was the moral panic experienced by mainstream adult culture with regard to some of the new youth trends, based on seemingly weird music, bizarre clothing, profane slang, and often strange lifestyles. In most cases, the moral panic was temporary; in others, it remained somewhat constant, as was the case with the goths for many years. Although the goth movement, too, eventually receded, in its heyday it carved out a lifestyle that set its adherents apart from both the mainstream culture and the subcultures of other youths. Another problematic subculture for many adults was the so-called geek one that emerged towards the end of the post-counterculture era itself—the geeks used their hacking abilities and their sarcastic wit to attack human conduct and social institutions effectively. Their descendants are Julian Assange of WikiLeaks and Edward Snowden, both of whom have gained notoriety by leaking sensitive information from governments and various institutions to the public.

A general characteristic of most of the emerging subcultures was the employment of irony, mockery, satire, and other "carnivalesque" modes of performance. The concept of the carnivalesque is traced to the late social critic Mikhail Bakhtin, and it is often enlisted to explain subcultures such as the punks and the goths.[1] An inherent aim of many of the new subcultures was an unconscious mocking of the social order. Unlike hippie culture, which wanted to dismantle the status quo, punks and cross-dressers like Alice Cooper aimed primarily to mock it and, like the carnival mockers of medieval times, to do so by donning outlandish costumes, employing crude language, and engaging in public acts considered to be vulgar and even obscene. In a sense, this strain of the new youth era could be traced to Mick Jagger's screaming rendition of "Satisfaction" (discussed in Chapter 3). Punk culture took that same kind of scream to greater extremes. Punk music was, in fact, essentially about the scream. As Bakhtin foresaw, carnivalesque forms of mockery, vulgarity, and screaming are self-satisfying and collectively therapeutic, leaving the social order largely intact and even validating it. Thus, while punk may have been perceived as a threat to mainstream mores, in the end, it did little to change them in radical ways. It mocked them and in so doing allowed young people to see through them.

Each subculture was represented, needless to say, by a distinct new musical style—disco, glam rock, punk rock, new wave, reggae, funk, etc. Three rose above the different fragments to garner relatively huge followings. They were disco, punk, and one that was based on the idea of sexual personae and cross-dressing. We will concentrate on these in this chapter, since it would be a gargantuan task to cover all the mutations that occurred in just the two decades after Woodstock. Initially associated with the gay lifestyle of New York City, disco drew upon black music (rhythm and blues, soul) to generate excitement in dance halls across the nation. It was a kind of throwback to the flapper dance hall and the rocker sock hop. Although despised by many other teens, disco had a substantial following in the 1970s, especially after the release of the motion picture *Saturday Night Fever* (1977) and its hugely successful soundtrack featuring the Bee Gees.

Around 1976, a punk subculture originated in London and New York in part as a reaction by disaffected youths against the commercialism of disco and the "artistic pretentiousness" of 1960s rock. Punk rock was raw, abrasive, and rude. It too was a throwback to the Rock Era, but specifically to its early brusqueness as evidenced by songs such as "Hound Dog" or "Tutti Frutti." But, unlike the 1950s rockers, punk bands such as the Sex Pistols and the Clash downplayed melody and harmony, emphasizing instead an angry, shrill, minimalist musical style and driving repetitive beat, meant to induce frenzy and a sense of disorder in audiences. Eventually, with such bands as Blondie and Talking Heads, punk developed softer and more melodious musical forms, called new wave, but its "screaming character" was the main gene in its constitution. Also in the mid-1970s, Jamaican reggae music started attracting attention among a sizable number of teens, after the release of the 1973 film *The Harder They Come*, which starred reggae singer Jimmy Cliff in the role of an underclass gangster. The superstar of reggae was, however, Bob Marley, who by the time of his death in 1981 had become an icon of the entire youth world.

The rise of popularity of reggae led to the emergence of rap culture a little later, after it influenced other musical styles and movements, including punk, which borrowed heavily from reggae. Bob Marley himself even recorded a song called "Punky Reggae Party" (1977). By 1986, rap culture had become dominant among young people. That was they year in which a hard rock band, Aerosmith, joined forces with a rap group, Run-D.M.C., to record "Walk This Way," showing the world that rap had merged with rock to produce a style that all youths could adopt as their own—hence a kind of retrieval of a singular *esprit* among young people.

Before the rap movement gained momentum, youth culture was in a quandary. In 1980, music sales plummeted and it appeared, for a little while at least, that the final chapter on it had been written. It was technology that came to the rescue. As mentioned, MTV, new possibilities for indie-production, and the introduction of the compact disc in 1983 revived interest in rock music. A new generation of "video rock stars," such as Michael Jackson, Prince, Bruce Springsteen, and Madonna, became icons of youth culture. The astronomical success of Jackson's 1982 *Thriller* video album contributed greatly to demonstrating the commercial value of video rock, as did the videos of heavy metal bands such as Van Halen, AC/DC, and Metallica. Their video performances were spectacular and evocative. Rock was back, thanks once again to technology.

As we saw, rock and roll became all the rage across the teen world after Elvis Presley appeared on *The Ed Sullivan Show* in

1956; and the same program catapulted the Beatles to international fame in 1964, when an estimated 73 million people watched the Beatles' first appearance on the show. Arguably, without television rock and other styles of youth music would have faded as quickly as they came onto the scene.[2] MTV was simply another phase in the historical partnership between the mass media and youth trends. However, things do come to an end. Rock is now moribund, especially if by that term we mean Elvis-style and counterculture music. Those styles appear to be increasingly objects of nostalgia. In 1995, the Rock and Roll Hall of Fame opened in Cleveland, Ohio—a sure sign that rock was already relegated to the category of "museum music." Also in the 1990s, several major television documentaries were produced on the history of rock and roll, and historical box-set recordings were reissued featuring rock artists from the past—further signs that rock music had indeed become more a nostalgic part of youth culture history than a continuing social force. But, on the other hand, the songs of Elvis, the Platters, and the Beatles are still around. And young people today seem to be discovering their dynamism, energy, and beauty. Perhaps the "music never did die," after the 1959 plane crash.

METAL

The starting point for any discussion of the post-counterculture era is metal music, which was the main, and arguably only, direct descendant of late hippie music. It combined earsplitting guitar sounds and shattering drum beats with Mick-Jagger-like screaming vocals. The music traced its roots to Jimi Hendrix. Early in his career, Hendrix played and toured with many famous rock performers, including Little Richard, who was the original 1950s screamer with songs like "Tutti Frutti," "Lucille," and "Good Golly Miss Molly." Hendrix gained fame after he moved to London and put out his first major album, *Are You*

Photo 4.1: Jimi Hendrix

Source: AF archive / Alamy Stock Photo

Experienced? (1967). His band, the Jimi Hendrix Experience, exploited heavily amplified guitar and bass to produce an inundation of sound, juxtaposed against an admixture of blues, psychedelic rock, and (in the ballads) more melodic elements, producing a unique sound. The guitar's "buzzing screech" was the feature that gave his music the name "hard rock." Hendrix's iconoclastic rendering of the American national anthem at Woodstock with his screaming guitar has left an indelible mark on social history.

It is both a mockery of the anthem and the injustices it encodes and a powerful emotional scream communicating the tormented lives of black people—the musical equivalent of Edvard Munch's overwhelming painting *The Scream*.

Metal rock as a distinct genre surfaced after the British group Led Zeppelin released four best-selling albums from 1969 to 1971. Metal culture expanded quickly after that, as bands such as Black Sabbath, Deep Purple, Grand Funk (also known as Grand Funk Railroad), Aerosmith, and Van Halen garnered large fanatical followings of young people. Their ear-shattering performances, distorted through deafening amplification, became the norm across all youth musical styles—and remain so to this day. The extended screeching, metallic guitar solos were also intrinsic to the style. Initially, the metal bands consisted only of male performers, emphasizing the testosterone alpha-male qualities of the hard rock style. The metal rocker look, too, was macho and rugged, consisting of ripped jeans, leather clothing, long flowing unkempt hair, beards, boots, buckles, T-shirts, and tattoos.

Though the early bands were critically reviled, a large slice of young people loved them just the same. They offered a clear alternative to late-hippie groups. By the mid-1970s, metal was spawning subgenres, with the mellower and musically eclectic sounds of Judas Priest and Motörhead. It was also receiving critical acclaim. The passionate fans who followed metal rock came to be known as "metalheads" or "headbangers." This referred to the fact that they would shake their heads furiously to the sounds of the band performing on stage in the so-called mosh pit, a spot near the stage where fans would congregate, headbang, push each other around, and often launch themselves into the crowd. They would also typically form the "devil's hand," with the index and little finger raised, symbolizing a salute to Satan.

By the early 1980s, metal was fragmenting even more into subgenres, of which "glam metal" attracted a fairly large following,

Photo 4.2: Led Zeppelin

Source: MARKA / Alamy Stock Photo

as did "thrash metal," a style that was extremely aggressive, as exemplified by groups such as Metallica and by mullet hairstyles. The metal musicians acted and looked like veritable "studs" on stage. Their lyrics were growled, not sung, conveying anger alongside machismo and its inherent bravado. It was a powerful stage act. Death metal and black metal also came to the surface, extolling gruesome satanic themes. Modern day offshoots of metal, such as "nu metal" and "metalcore" are more eclectic, combining elements from funk, hip-hop, and punk.

In the main metal culture was macho theatre, even though women metal bands eventually came onto the scene displaying as much machismo, if not more, than their male counterparts. The phallic symbolism built into the overall musical and performative script, including stroking the guitar aggressively in simulation of penile stroking, was unmistakable. The metal ballads, on the other hand, were paradoxically sensual, romantic, and even spiritual. This is saliently evident in Led Zeppelin's classic 1973 song "Stairway to Heaven," which combines both aspects—the macho and the spiritual. The song thus blends melodic poignancy in the slow opening part with increasing hard rock feel in the second and third parts.

As the metal movement showed once again, youth culture has always been an equal-opportunity culture, with males and females participants in it. Even in the 1950s, women rock stars like Annette Funicello and Connie Francis were superstars with both male and female fans. This was also the pattern, as we saw, in the Roaring Twenties, when black women jazz singers came onto the scene, alongside male performers, to the chagrin and even terror of the staid society of the era—a fact emphasized by the movie *Chicago* in which women literally "ran the show" and where men were reduced to secondary and irrelevant roles. By assuming a macho style, the metal women were even more threatening on the stage than were the men. They further advanced the gender-role-bashing process started by previous youth movements.

Crucial to the overall metal look was tattooing. Tattooing is ancient. Cave paintings date it as far back as 8000 BCE. In early civilizations, it was associated not with criminality but regality. In ancient Egypt, tattooing was reserved, in fact, for the nobility. It was the ancient Greeks and Romans who used tattoos to brand slaves and criminals. Tattooing became attractive to sailors, who saw it as part of their macho image. Tattoos became membership symbols of motorcycle gangs, remaining so to this day among various criminal groups such as the Russian Mafia and the Yakuza. Prisoners have also used tattoos as signs of toughness and fearsomeness for decades. The adoption of tattooing as a youth trend began with metal culture in the early 1970s. A little later, the Rolling Stones made it a society-wide fad with their popular 1981 album *Tattoo You*. Today, tattooing has evolved into a cosmetic trend, having lost most, if not all, of the macho symbolism with which it originally resonated among metalheads.

Another aspect of metal culture was occultism (discussed already in the previous chapter). The same trend was picked up by and spread even more broadly later by "shock-rocker" Marilyn Manson and others. All this caused, as expected, moral panic on the part of society at large, and especially on the part of conservative politicians and religious leaders. The practice that most got their attention was so-called backwards masking, or the supposed insertion of satanic messages in a record. The demonic message supposedly became audible only when the record was played backwards. The most famous case in point was, ironically, Led Zeppelin's haunting and powerful "Stairway to Heaven" (mentioned above) in which the line "your stairway lies on the whispering wind" was claimed to be actually "cause I live with Satan" in reverse. Maybe the band did indeed cleverly embed that phrase as the social guardians at the time suspected; maybe not. The occultist trend spread more because of the moral panic. Once something is forbidden, it takes on a vigorous life of its own among young people.

Were metal groups such as Black Sabbath serious about their devil worship or were they using it simply as a parodic element in their stage persona? As mentioned in the previous chapter, the very same fascination with magic, wizardry, satanism, astrology, and other occult themes was part of the hippie code. The hippie engagement with occult themes, however, harboured a deeper reason than social satire and mockery. It was their replacement for traditional religion in the Age of Aquarius. Carl Jung referred to practices such as occultism as manifestations of the Shadow archetype.[3] The need to "escape the prison house of the flesh," as Gary Lachman has put it, has often been satisfied by occult practices and traditions.[4] It should come as no surprise, therefore, that the Shadow archetype remade its appearance in death metal.

PUNK

As metal culture was expanding, some young people started turning their attention elsewhere. A new trend was the cult movie phenomenon *The Rocky Horror Picture Show* (1977), that had hordes of teenagers going to see it day after day, week after week, month after month. It was both a parody of 1950s rock and roll culture and an acknowledgment that mockery itself was becoming a major force within youth culture generally. As Greenwald put it, it was both an attempt "to shock by departing from the tradition of rock and roll machismo established by Elvis" and "an overall smearing of the lines between the generations and the sexes."[5]

It was in the same time frame that punk rock entered the scene, with such bands as Blondie, the Ramones, Television, the Patti Smith Group, the Sex Pistols, the Clash, and X-Ray Spex, among others. These groups adopted the transgressive mocking images of *Rocky Horror* but gave them a much harder defiant edge. The punks were mockers, deliberately trying to offend their own audiences, in a self-immolating way, with their use of profanity and disgusting actions on stage. The overall act appealed broadly, with many disenchanted youths joining in, dressing and behaving like the band members, including reversed dog collars, symbols of non-compliance, and strange hairdos, with both sides of the head shaved completely, leaving a strip of longer hair spiked with gel so that it stands up.

Photo 4.3: The Punk Look

Source: Photo by Grant Mitchell, Flickr, CC BY 2.0

The punk look, walk, and talk smacked of "stick-it-in-your face" anti-authoritarian defiance tinged with bravado. The Clash and the Gang of Four, among others, introduced lyrics that were, at the time, unprecedented in their vulgarity. But, in the end, the movement was not as politically effective as was the counterculture one, primarily because punk culture was an introverted one; that is, the punks didn't care about changing mainstream society; they were focused on themselves and their fans. Other youths looked upon punk lifestyle as something ludicrous, bordering on the comical. The leather collars with sharp spikes protruding from them were a perfect example of this. Originally, such collars were designed for dog training. The spikes protruded inwards as part of negative conditioning. If the dog disobeyed a command, the leash, attached to its collar, would be pulled, thus punishing the dog by driving the spikes into its neck. Being against all forms of authority and social conditioning, the punks reversed the dog collar in parody of such obedience training. The protruding spikes, therefore, symbolized a reversal of power alignments, signaling that the wearer would never be controlled by society. To outsiders, however, they seemed just silly; the social nuances of the collar simply escaped most people.

Such items of clothing are elements of so-called confrontation dress—a clothing code designed to subvert the meanings of everyday props. Razor blades, tampons, and safety pins used as jewelry by the punks were further examples of this type of dress. Ironically and paradoxically, cooption occurred here as it did in the hippie era. The business world took some of these confrontational props and turned them into fashion items, a sure sign that punk's subversiveness was being tamed. In acknowledgement of their sell-out, the Sex Pistols reunion tour in 1996 was labelled, the Filthy Lucre Tour, as shares in the venture were floated on the British stock exchange.

Despite the cooption, the punk movement did not completely disappear. It started morphing into subcultures, such as new wave and alternative. The new artists were hardly confrontational or abrasive as their predecessors were. They were more mainstream, and included Elvis Costello, the Cure, Talking Heads, and the Cars. As culture theorist Dick Hebdige has argued, this should come as no surprise because, once a subculture becomes visible to all in a society, its code becomes commodified, attenuated, and thus enucleated of its symbolic power.[6] This happened the instant punk dress was peddled as fashion exotica by clothiers. New wave groups such as the B-52s and New Order even blended punk style with dance music—an absolute oxymoron if there ever was one. The Police recorded best-selling albums *Ghost in the Machine* (1981) and *Synchronicity* (1983), which included the hit "Every Breath You Take" by the group's lead singer Sting, who later had a successful solo career.

Talking Heads, U2, whose 1987 album *The Joshua Tree* sold millions of copies worldwide, and other bands were no longer seen as threats to the social order. Punk had been truly tamed, becoming absorbed by the mainstream.

By late 1980s and early 1990s, through such bands as Nirvana, Pearl Jam, and Soundgarden, all originating in Seattle, punk started morphing even more drastically, mutating into grunge and other emerging hard sounds, which had become so different that their punk genealogy was completely lost. Nirvana, the first grunge group to reach a wide audience, exploded onto the music scene with its second album, *Nevermind* (1991). A hit MTV video for one of the songs on the album, "Smells Like Teen Spirit," helped Nirvana gain a huge following. The group broke up in 1994 after its lead vocalist, Kurt Cobain, committed suicide at age 27 after recovering from a drug-induced coma earlier that year. Nine Inch Nails, an American alternative rock group, mixed angry lyrics with heavy metal sounds and synthesized electronic music. Other alternative groups and artists originating in the 1990s included Green Day; No Doubt, which incorporated Jamaican popular music called ska into their sound; the Prodigy, which combined aggressive messages with a hard-driving dance beat; and Oasis, a British group that adopted a Beatles-style melodic and harmonic structure to a basic punk beat. The original punk genes had, clearly, mutated considerably.

Another subculture of the era, loosely connected to new wave, was the so-called emo one. The word *emo* is short for "emotional hardcore." It was championed by bands such as Minor Threat, which was previously a straightedge hardcore band. Over time, the genre evolved and moved in a more pop-punk direction, creating an independent and short-lived emo subculture.

Like punks, emos rejected all other forms of teen culture as well as mainstream society. The main difference between emo and punk was the fact that emo emphasized emotions in the music, on stage, and in enclave gatherings. Emo youths glorified suffering, depression, and even self-harm. They were often treated as outcasts by peers. So, they immersed themselves into their own subculture, which allowed them to validate their suffering and isolation through music. In a sense, the emos took psychotherapy into their own hands by proclaiming to the world, "I am who I am; you may reject me; but I belong to something that is meaningful."

It is relevant to note that the purported threat posed by the punks was foreshadowed in Stanley Kubrick's cinematic masterpiece of 1971, *A Clockwork Orange*, in which a deranged youth—a forerunner of the apathetic, dangerous punk persona—is the central figure in the movie.

The setting for the movie is 1970s Britain. A teenage thug, Alex De Large, perpetrates a daily routine of crime and sex in a wanton and reckless fashion. Caught and imprisoned for murder, he volunteers to undergo an experimental shock treatment therapy that brainwashes him to become nauseated by his previous lifestyle. Mr. Alexander, an author and one of Alex's victims, entraps him with the aim of avenging himself. He hopes to drive Alex to commit suicide, ironically, to the strains of Beethoven's Ninth Symphony—the total antithesis to punk music. But Alex is supported by the press and soon after he is released and restored to health. The movie ends with no true conclusion. But the scenario of senseless, aimless violence that a teenager is capable of perpetrating has a profound warning in it. Alex is a portrait of a goalless and ruthless teen trapped in a weary, decaying environment. His only way out is through intimidation and physicality. He is a ticking time bomb ready to explode at any instant. Alex, like Holden Caulfield in *The Catcher in the Rye*, feels an acute and urgent need to change— indeed to "save"—the world. But unlike Holden he does it in a physically destructive manner. The rage in Alex's eyes was the rage shown by the early punks.

Photo 4.4: Malcolm McDowell as Alex De Large in
A Clockwork Orange
Source: AF archive / Alamy Stock Photo

GOTH

One of the earliest mutations of punk culture was called "goth." The early goths were an occultist shadow culture, more so than were the death metal bands and their hippie predecessors. The goth appearance consisted of black eyeliner, lipstick, fishnet stockings (worn or cut), black boots, black hair, and other dark-shaded accouterments and cosmetic decorations. The origins of goth are summarized succinctly by Jillian Venters as follows:

> The Goth subculture as it is known today began as an offshoot of punk rock that mixed a flair for the theatrical and a fondness of campy horror movies. While every cultural movement or phase has cast its own dark shadows

(vampy flappers and sinister rakes, noir femmes fatales, black-clad occult types reading tarot cards by candlelight), those shadows never really seemed to flow together into a glorious tapestry of velvet-edged darkness in the U.K. and U.S. until the late '70s and early '80s.[7]

Goth culture had its tentacles in various cultural reflexes, including Gothic literature, the works of Edgar Allan Poe, Batman, television series such as *The Addams Family*, and especially in *The Rocky Horror Picture Show*. The latter requires further commentary here, since it undoubtedly influenced both the punk and early goth movements. *Rocky Horror* debuted in 1975 in Britain. From the start, it was carnival mockery at its best, ridiculing and lampooning traditional gender roles, mainstream culture fashion practices, and the pseudo-morality of society. It continues on as a kind of Halloween tradition in many areas of the contemporary world, taking place at midnight, with patrons showing up dressed in drag and lingerie. As in the medieval carnivals, the audience is not only part of the show, it is the show—dancing and singing, shouting lewd comments at the screen, and throwing objects at certain points in the film, such as toast, toilet paper, water, or rice. The master of ceremonies, called ironically Dr. Frank-N-Furter, instructs and exhorts the audience with the following words:

> Give yourself over to absolute pleasure. Swim the warm waters of sins of the flesh—erotic nightmares beyond any measure, and sensual daydreams to treasure forever. Can't you just see it? Don't dream it, be it.

To his entreaty, audience members start to indulge themselves in "absolute pleasure," drinking alcohol, smoking, and often groping each other sexually. *Rocky Horror* never made it into mainstream movie theatres because it was too weird and

Photo 4.5: A Goth Youth

Source: Photo by Bryan Ledgard, Flickr, CC BY 2.0

overtly transgressive. But it made it into the hearts of the youths of that era, who were dissatisfied with hippie culture and with new trends. *Rocky Horror*'s dystopic symbolism became a reflex in the ethos of both punk and goth, with men wearing corsets and fishnet stockings, women displaying themselves in blatant sexual ways, and Dr. Frank-N-Furter's animated sex-toy in the form of a corpse becoming a veritable ironic statement. The use of the word *Horror* in the spectacle is significant. The horror genre, like occultism generally, taps into a fear of the grotesque and the unknown. From the zombie films of the 1950s and 1960s to current day gory films like the *Hostel* and *Saw* sets of films, horror provides a cathartic escape from inner horrors and the fear of nihilism. As British film critic Robin Wood aptly observes, "One might say that the true subject of the horror genre is the struggle for recognition of all that our civilization represses and oppresses," including our inability to face our "nothingness and probable purposelessness."[8]

Rocky Horror's appeal to the goths was unmistakable. They quickly became an "apart" culture—that is, one that lived completely apart from the mainstream, with their own periodicals, clubs, language, courtship rituals, and so on and so forth. They married mainly within the group and had baby goths with the goal of extending the culture beyond one generation. The goths became, in other words, a self-sustaining autonomous culture, later using the Internet to keep their community alive. As sociologist Paul Hodkinson aptly puts it: "Far from distracting them into other interests or dissolving the boundaries of their subculture, the internet usually functioned, in the same way as goth events, to concentrate their involvement in the goth scene and to reinforce the boundaries of the grouping."[9] As a parallel (or apart) culture, goth has lasted longer than most other cultures that originated among young people. But it too has virtually vanished in the twenty-first century, for reasons to be discussed in the final chapter.

The Rocky Horror Picture Show also left its residues in shock and cross-dressing trends in the late 1970s and early 1980s. For example, the members of the rock band Kiss assumed mock comic-book roles—a glamour boy, an alien from outer space, a kitty cat, and a sex-crazed Kabuki monster. Band members wore makeup, and their stage act included fire-eating, smoke-bombs, hydraulic lifts, and the smashing of instruments. All this brings us back to Mikhail Bakhtin's notion of the carnivalesque.[10] The festivities associated with carnival, Bakhtin argued, are a celebration of chaos. They exalt the body and its urges at the same time that they mock the sacred order through insults and caricaturizations of authority figures. Carnival is a celebration of the god Chaos, who looks over enactments and rituals that are intended to mock, ridicule, laugh at, and scorn everything that is sacred and authoritative. Carnival, in any of its forms, from the Roman Saturnalia to the Mardi Gras of New Orleans, has been an intrinsic part of popular and folkloristic traditions from time immemorial, allowing common people to indulge in behaviour that would otherwise be viewed as illegal or immoral and punished as such. Rather than truly disrupt tradition and threaten existing social norms, carnivals allow people to theatricalize their revulsion of the rigidity intrinsic in the sacred order, and especially its taboos on the body. From this, there have emerged carnivalesque genres that have allowed artists, thinkers, and common people alike to mock the lofty notions of the sacred order. Comedy, satire, parody, mimicry, and other forms of expression designed to evoke laughter—the opposite of seriousness—are manifestations of the carnivalesque instinct. Bakhtinian theory provides us with a truly insightful framework for understanding the patterns in youth culture that emerged in the post-hippie era.

SEXUAL PERSONAE

In her controversial book, titled *Sexual Personae*, the acerbic cultural critic Camille Paglia showed that the sexual-gender roles we assume are artifacts of history, not products of nature, much like Michel Foucault had argued in his assessment of the history of sexual ideologies.[11] *The Rocky Horror Picture Show* mocked our historically acquired models of sexual normalcy, based on heterosexuality, and our insistence on maintaining gender differentiations at all levels of society. Indeed, *Rocky Horror* implicitly suggested that we would all wear different sexual personae if they were not so harshly repressed. Shortly after *Rocky Horror*, a "sexual personae movement," as it can be called, was spearheaded by various artists of the era, including Alice Cooper, the members of Kiss, David Bowie, Madonna, Prince, Marilyn Manson, and Michael Jackson, among others. Madonna in particular became a kind of leader in this movement, donning a new and powerful sexual persona that straddled various previous

Photo 4.6: Madonna

Source: United Archives GmbH / Alamy Stock Photo

traditions of femininity and womanhood: "I have the same goal I've had ever since I was a girl. I want to rule the world."[12] As Camille Paglia argued, performances such as those by Madonna revealed a "sexual power that feminism cannot explain and has tried to destroy,"[13] which nonetheless "expresses women's ancient and eternal control of the sexual realm," and "stalks all men's relations with women."[14]

In her "material girl" persona, which she adopted in her hit song "Material Girl" (1985), Madonna put on display the power of the sexual female persona. The song was from her classic album *Like a Virgin* (1984)—a double-entendre on her name. The album became the first one by a woman artist to sell more than 7 million copies. Madonna's bold lyrics and flashy costumes gave her a salacious image, which she constructed as part of her persona, mixing sexual and religious elements in it. Her 1992 album *Erotica* and a book of photographs of her called *Sex* (1992) stirred additional controversy, as she further entrenched her sexual persona into the public imagination.

Her concerts were literally "spectacular"—the word *spectacle* derives from Latin *spectare*, which means "to look at." They were very much like the "peep shows" of the carnival sideshows. Using the power of her femininity she invited *spectare* from both male and female audiences. Her intermingling of the sacred and the profane in videos such as "Like a Prayer"—an obvious parodic allusion to *Like a Virgin*—was all about the power of sexual spectacle in both carnivals and religions. Not unlike early tribal rituals, her spectacles combined these two dimensions in order to bring out the tension that exists between them.

Madonna's sexual persona was strongly heterosexual, but it also had lesbian tinges to it. Indeed, she open-mouth kissed Britney Spears at the 2003 MTV Video Music Awards, playing on the subtext of bisexuality (in a public way).

Madonna actually turned the tide in favour of a "freer womanhood," spearheading the movement known as post-feminism.[15] She did this by exposing the latent hypocritical puritanism and suffocating white middle-class view of American academic feminism. There is little doubt that the so-called girl power movement, exemplified by British rock band the Spice Girls, took its cue from Madonna.

Madonna's influence on white gender politics extended to African American politics as well. Feminist author bell hooks sees in Madonna's sexual persona a racial political subtext—a subtext that Madonna brings out powerfully:

> For masses of black women, the political reality that underlies Madonna's own recognition that in a society where "blondes" not only "have more fun" but where they are more likely to succeed in any endeavor is white supremacy and racism... In this sense Madonna has much in common with the masses of black women who suffer from internalized racism and are forever terrorized by a standard of beauty they feel they can never truly embody.[16]

Following on Madonna's coattails was gender-bending culture, symbolized best by the late Michael Jackson. Jackson spent his childhood performing with his family band, the Jackson Five, a group that performed a mixture of rock and disco. Jackson found stardom as an adult with his best selling albums *Off the Wall* (1979) and *Thriller* (1982), the latter becoming the biggest selling album in music history at the time, selling over 45 million copies. The music video of the song "Thriller" is a 13-minute horror flick that combines singing and dancing with spectacular visual and sound effects.

Jackson also had hits with his dance-heavy videos "Billie Jean" and "Beat It" (both 1983). Jackson's hero was Elvis Presley, a macho rocker if there ever was one—ironic given the ambiguous

Photo 4.7: Michael Jackson

Source: Trinity Mirror / Mirrorpix / Alamy Stock Photo

sexual persona that Jackson adopted. Both Michael Jackson and Madonna became youth celebrities in large part because they tapped into a new consciousness about sex and gender that was fomenting in society at large. With his many eccentricities, Jackson extolled both male and female sexual characteristics at once, as well as black and white racial qualities (achieved through extensive cosmetic surgery to his face). Jackson straddled the sexual fence, tantalizing his audiences to join him on either the homosexual or bisexual sides. Whether it is themes like masturbation in his hit "Beat It," or androgyny in his late 1980s album *Bad*, Michael Jackson was a deconstructionist of traditional sexuality. He gave symbolic expression to gender-bending more powerfully than did Alice Cooper or Marilyn Manson. He did it because he was hugely popular with all teens, not just a subsection of them.

DISCO

Running totally against all the above-mentioned trends in the post-counterculture era was disco culture. Its popularity with hordes of teens was further evidence of youth culture's mutation. Disco teens were vastly different from their punk, goth, and cross-dressing counterparts. Their lifestyle was based on dancing and having fun. Punk teens rejected disco culture with the expression "disco sucks!" So too did other teens, who saw the disco scene as too superficial and much too acceptable to the adult world. But disco thrived nonetheless, because it was fun and sexy.

Disco culture actually emerged in the late 1960s, gaining momentum in the mid-1970s. It was a throwback to the Roaring Twenties and the swing dance mania of the 1930s and 1940s, reintroducing the vogue of ballroom dancing into youth culture, which hippie, metal, punk, and goth culture had virtually eliminated, as they looked down upon it as frivolous. Only

Madonna and Michael Jackson revived dancing as part of their spectacles; otherwise it had virtually disappeared from the youth social radar screen. Disco music was characterized by a steady infectious beat that got people to go onto the floor and dance the night away. The success of the motion picture *Saturday Night Fever* (1977), starring John Travolta, popularized disco more broadly and brought about a so-called clubbing phenomenon. As Ben Malbon puts it, "Whether the clubbing crowd is actually diverse in terms of identities or not, what matters is that many clubbers understand the clubbing crowd, of which they are a part, to be diversely constituted, and they crucially find this understanding a rewarding and enriching experience."[17]

Disco was a pagan-style celebration of the body in motion. The title of the movie captured the essence of what the Saturday night party-dance scene had become among teenagers—a feverish need to be with one's peers engaged in sexually suggestive dancing. The disco scene was an unabashed hedonistic rite purified culturally by the glitter and glitz of high fashion. Bands and performers like Chic, the Village People, Donna Summer, and KC and the Sunshine Band and catered to the "feverish instincts" of primarily affluent, middle-class teenagers. It was seen by many other teens as superficial and meaningless socially.

The tension between punk and disco was captured magnificently by Spike Lee in his 1999 movie *Summer of Sam*, which takes place in the summer of 1977 during the height of the Son of Sam serial murders. The main subtext in the movie was the acerbic contrast between punk and disco culture. It is thus no surprise that music plays a prominent role in the film, with the contrast between punk and disco styles being highly evocative and compelling. The movie thus provides an insightful commentary on the society of the times and, more generally, on American society—a society guided by fads and subcultures, rather than by a common "dream," as the mythology of

Photo 4.8: John Travolta and Karen Lynn Gorney in
Saturday Night Fever (1977)

Source: Movie poster for the film *Saturday Night Fever,* ScreenProd /
Photononstop / Alamy Stock Photo

America would have us believe. Derivatives of disco included techno, now EDM, and especially the DJ phenomenon, which need not concern us here.

Disco has left its imprint in tamer ways on youth culture, and mainstream culture generally. It can be seen, for instance, in the revival of ballroom dancing on television and in music halls throughout the first decade of the 2000s.

RAVE

Disco lasted until nearly the early 1990s, when a new movement emerged that gained broad popularity—a movement that attempted to revive the hippie happening, with its powerful admixture of music and drugs to heighten the bonding experience of the group. It was called "rave." Like punk and goth, it was transgressive of social norms, offering youths an environment for establishing solidarity through drugs, dance, and raucous music. Like all carnivalesque subcultures, its aim was not revolution; it was substitution—the substitution of hypocritical social attitudes with more realistic ones. So far, nothing was new, since the hippies had a similar view of life, going even further by protesting and demanding change. The difference was the extreme tribalism inherent in the rave scene, where the drug ecstasy became the main component of the ritual. Rave culture, ironically, grew out of the disco scene when club DJs in American cities began experimenting with different sounds. Known as the Acid House movement, it started to alter the original sounds of disco recordings with electronic technologies. This allowed them to control the musical tempo so as to get the dancers to move in various random ways.[18] This new form of "electronic disco" gradually spawned its own subgenres, such as house and techno.[19]

As the music grew in popularity, fans began to organize large dance parties that came to be known as raves, at which ecstasy was consumed.[20] These were held in warehouses, fields, and airplane hangars, or other places that were out of view of the authorities for obvious reasons. Adding to the secrecy was the tactic of announcing the locale of the rave just a few hours before the rave itself.[21] The dress code was the admission ticket. It consisted basically of a late-hippie look, with standard jeans and T-shirt (the T-shirt generally carrying drug-related messages or symbols).[22] Also part of the code were glow sticks, hot pants, soothers, and whistles.

The rave was a modern-day Dionysian feast. Dionysus, the god of wine, was a deity who inspired ecstatic, orgiastic worship. The term *orgy* has become connected with unrestrained sexual activity, but its origins are much less licentious. In Greek, *orgia* meant "secret rites, worship," and was used with reference to the rites practised in the worship of Dionysus. These included, above all else, dancing and drinking. The rave was a Dionysian event, with its loud pulsating bass accompaniment and repetitive beats, inducing the ravers into a trance-like bacchanalian state, heightened by the drug ecstasy (a rather appropriate name). It was a celebration of the body, a means of defusing its sexual urges and giving them a channel for diffusion and sublimation. As Brian Ott and Bill Herman observe, it was "the interaction of music, DJ, and ravers, in which no element was more or less important than the rest."[23] Like the hippies, ravers developed a lifestyle code based on peace, love, unity, and respect.[24] Inevitably, rave culture caused moral panic, bringing about calls for the authorities to step in and stop the raves. As raves relocated to legitimate clubs and other regulated venues, the culture started losing its tribal appeal. Although snippets of rave culture are still around, it has virtually disappeared as a distinct one, having evolved into a general club culture.

EPILOGUE

The theme of mutation was, as announced at the start of this chapter, the framework for analyzing the post-counterculture or Electronic Era. Mutations occurred in many ways, as we have seen. These included even a new global form of youth culture, characterized by movements such as the "Another World" one, which crystallized from a combination of rock, disco, punk, and music from other cultures. The English rocker Peter Gabriel, a former lead singer of Genesis, and David Byrne, the vocalist of Talking Heads, interspliced African, Latin American, and Middle Eastern elements onto a metal rock musical frame.

The world was obviously in a deconstruction mood, an idea put forth by the late French philosopher Jacques Derrida.[25] Although it is improbable that the youths of the era read the works on deconstruction theory, they certainly tapped into the larger social Zeitgeist that was unfolding and that had actually been started by the hippies. The main idea in deconstruction is that the meaning of a text, such as a religious one, cannot be determined because it shifts according to who analyzes it, when it is analyzed, and how it is analyzed. There is no "authoritative" or "natural" interpretation to the text. Rather, every text has inbuilt perspectives in it that come from specific historical traditions, and these are imprinted in the words and themes used. Texts are not mirrors of reality; they are mirrors of the biases and prejudices of their makers. Challenging authority, therefore, is challenging the hegemony of authorship. Alice Cooper, Kiss, Marilyn Manson and others like them were deconstructionists, showing in their own way that meaning is a socially constrained phenomenon. Being male or female is also a construction; Madonna, Michael Jackson, and others showed this by deconstructing gender, assuming different sexual personae. Sacred culture (the culture where authorship is deemed to be definitive to the interpretation of texts) is nothing but a system of "ideologies," not a means of understanding "reality." Cooper's 1975 concept album *Welcome to My Nightmare* was his way of articulating what it means to be a part of the "other side" where people can realize that received truth is an illusion. It is part of a "nightmare" where laughing and screaming are the means for coming to grips with reality.

In Chinese philosophy, there is a basic notion called the *yin* and *yang*—two opposing forces that are believed to combine in various proportions to produce a balance in the different moods experienced by humans. The process of creating balance was called purification by Bakhtin. Early punk bands, such as the Sex Pistols, sang about the grotesque nature of bodies. One of their slogans was "F... Forever!" alluding to sex as a simple animal act. The band also made fun of the monarchy, the government, the human body, multinational corporations, and styles of tamer rock. The function of their performances was that of purification. Through crude, bawdy, and vulgar performances and rituals, the grotesque within us is sublimated. In the end, such forms of vulgarity are innocuous. They become dangerous only if they are repressed politically. Fortunately that did not happen. While punk rock created moral panic, it never really had a disruptive impact on the social mainstream. After purification, the sacred is restored.

CHAPTER 5

Integration: Rap and Hip-Hop

Hip-hop has done so much for racial relations, and I don't think it's given the proper credit. It has changed America immensely. I'm going to make a very bold statement: Hip-hop has done more than any leader, politician, or anyone to improve race relations.

—Jay-Z (b. 1969)

PROLOGUE

It is no coincidence that during the last few days of the acerbic and controversial 2016 campaign for American president, Hillary Clinton, the Democratic candidate, had rappers like Jay-Z come out in full support of her candidacy, hosting concerts to help bolster her chances of winning. In the end, all such efforts failed and the repercussions, politically and racially, will be studied ad infinitum. But the fact that a presidential candidate sought to ally herself with iconic representatives of the hip-hop movement showed that the latter had truly made an impact on society in its overall attempt at improving race relations, as Jay-Z put it in the above epigraph, that is of finally achieving the true integration of blacks and whites. On the other hand, the neglect of black voters by many politicians during the campaign showed, ominously, that this may have been just idealistic thinking, and that racism was not yet vanquished. It was lurking just below the surface of the political theatre.

The rap movement came to the forefront in the 1990s. It was an attempt by African American musicians, at first, to come to grips with their impoverished and underprivileged conditions, especially in urban centres; it was, in its own way, a second counterculture and civil rights movement. It was not a mutation, like other post-counterculture movements discussed in the previous chapter were. It stood apart from all the other subcultures of the era in a specific way—it constituted an unprecedented attempt to validate African American history, suffering, and identity on its own terms. In the process, it produced some of the most powerful musical ideas and works of the post-counterculture era.

As a distinct style, rap traces its roots to the late 1970s. Its popularity, especially among young African Americans, grew quickly. Its infectious beat and its transgressive rhyming lyrics were contagious. By 1985, rap had its first super group, Run-D.M.C., whose 1984 album, *Run-D.M.C.*, became a gold album. That moment signalled a new and interesting turn in youth culture—a turn that took place two years later in 1986. That was year when the iconic metal band Aerosmith performed with Run-D.M.C. and recorded the hit song "Walk This Way." The song said it all. Combining elements of metal and rap, it heralded the arrival of a new strain in youth culture, with an exciting "walk" to it. The lyrics encapsulated this perfectly, with the attitude imprinted in a worldview that harked back to the Flapper Era in many ways. "Hip," an ingredient in both the Beat writers' "hipsterism" and in "hippie" culture was back with a brash new stance and posture. As the song phrased it, it was all about the "hey diddle diddle" that characterized the new "walk."

The style of the lyrics exuded hipsterism at its most rudimentary and appealing, breaking rules of grammar ("knowed") and social propriety ("missy") intentionally. The subtext was clear—this new blend of rock and rap would empower everyone, not just African Americans; it would symbolically integrate the past with the present, the world of metal rock with the world of rap, black with white. The verve of that emblematic song spread like wildfire. After that, rap became a dominant movement in youth culture generally, attracting more and more people to it from all races and backgrounds. It thus embraced "integration," both in musical styles and among the races. By the late 1990s, rap held a hegemonic status in the world of youth culture, as it became increasingly eclectic, reflecting its heritage in soul and blues more and more and, indirectly, moving away from the "walk." Artists like Lauryn Hill started mixing rap and soul in new aesthetically interesting ways. Her first solo album, *The Miseducation of Lauryn Hill* (1998), won five Grammy Awards. The Black Eyed Peas, Alicia Keys, and others followed suit. Although artistically marvelous, these very trends took rap away from its initial aims, leading to its fade-out in the late 2000s. There is still a rap culture today, but it has lost its original vivacious "walk." Like other youth movements of the past, it is now more of an option than a compulsion for teens.

Why rap? When it barged onto the scene, it heralded a new vibrant form of rebellion, evoking the same kind of defiant mood of counterculture youths in the 1960s. The counterculture movement had made inroads into the elimination of racism; but the work was not finished. The revolution was taken on by the rap movement. The beat was elemental, almost primal, and thus subconsciously and archetypally powerful. The overall message was brashly subversive; it spawned a different lifestyle, called hip-hop, which consisted of a new language, clothing (baggy pants, ultra long-sleeved shirts and jackets), unlaced sneakers, neck chains, earrings, and toques. The image was one of "gangsta" toughness. Wearing pants with the crotch near the knees was particularly symbolic of this. For safety reasons, prisoners are not allowed to wear belts, so they are forced to wear their pants low, and rappers adopted this "style." The connection to prison life was unmistakable, if only vicariously or via verisimilitude. Reflecting the real life on the streets of poverty and imprisonment in urban ghettos, and the need to cope with this reality through music and dress, the hip-hop code was a coping mechanism for many young African Americans, and an empowering one at that. The gangsta brash attitude, with its frontal (in-your-face) assault on society—and especially the police—was visibly confrontational.

Rappers such as Tupac Shakur, Dr. Dre, members of Wu-Tang Clan, and Notorious B.I.G. to name a few, used highly explicit lyrics advocating violence, the use of drugs, blatant sexuality, and the use of weapons. But the lyrics, the symbols, the threats, the images were, in the end, part of a desperate cry for change—a need for "integration" at all levels. The rap movement was, in a phrase, a condemnation of racial discrimination; it was a voice of conscience telling America that something was wrong, desperately wrong.

ORIGINS

Jazz, blues, gospel, swing, boogie-woogie, and bebop prepared the groundwork for rock and roll to emerge in the 1950s, as we saw. The same musical lineage can be seen in the genetic makeup of early rap, which was (at least initially) a musical "escape valve" from social conditions, producing a fun-seeking spirit, as did jazz and rock and roll. However, as it evolved, its mood became more serious, and the dancing receded to the background. In 1982, for example, Grandmaster Flash and the Furious Five used the rap medium to take a hard critical look at social issues, portraying the dreadful plight of black inner-city residents on *The Message*. Public Enemy and Ice Cube subsequently popularized styles and approaches to rap that were more militant and radical than most previous youth movements, at least on the surface.

Rap traces its heritage to the dance clubs of Jamaica in the 1970s. In those clubs, disc jockeys talked over the records they played, performing a kind of rhythmic and on-the-spot poetic vocalization, accompanied by music snippets, called samples, from pre-recorded material or from music created on purpose. This became the basic rap style over an elemental beat that connected perfectly with the lyrics. The early songs were thus based on a vocalized or chanted style of music. Melody and harmony were supportive of the beat, rather than guiding it. Perhaps the early rappers wanted to break radically from the melodious black music of the past, such as the kind of music sung by Ray Charles, Nat King Cole, the Platters, and the Drifters, which they may have seen as catering too much to white tastes. Whatever the reason, rap had a unique new style that was unprecedented in youth culture. It had descendants, but like any compound, the whole was bigger than the sum of its parts.

Photo 5.1: The Sugarhill Gang

Source: Pictorial Press Ltd / Alamy Stock Photo

Rap was imported to the nightclubs of New York a little later in the 1970s. Eventually, it led to a full-blown new type of music there. The first rap records were made in the mid to late 1970s. They were put out at first mainly by small, independent record companies, although already in 1979, rapper Kurtis Blow signed with a major label and had a gold record within a year. Rap had arrived. The Sugarhill Gang recorded the first major rap anthem, "Rapper's Delight," in the same year of 1979.

Photo 5.2: Break Dancing

Source: Photo courtesy of Wikimedia Commons

The genre did not really catch on with youths generally until 1986 and "Walk This Way" came along. By the end of the 1980s, rap culture started expanding astronomically across all youth demographics. As evidence, MTV established a program dedicated solely to rap, and the records of rap artists such as MC Hammer and the Beastie Boys achieved multi-platinum status. Radio stations devoted exclusively to rap started cropping up all over America and the world for that matter. As in the case of rock and roll, the rest of the world was listening and jumped on the bandwagon with their own local versions of rap. The art of rap artists, such as Public Enemy, and LL Cool J, became influential throughout the music universe by the mid-1990s.

From the outset, rap was essentially dance music. The dances were performed, at first, and rather vigorously, in the streets by so-called break dancers. They were a type of street urchins who caught everyone's attention with their acrobatic dancing to the infectious beat of the music.

But this situation changed when the music caught on broadly. Rap was no longer for break dancers; it was part of a new musical idiom inveighing against systemic injustices. It was, in effect, an implicit civil rights movement. The music generated controversy initially among both white and black adult Americans, since it dealt abrasively with social issues, as well as adopting a brassy, almost pornographic, approach to sex. "Cop Killer," a 1992 song by Ice-T's band Body Count, for example, talked about murdering police officers. Outraged parents and public officials boycotted the album and put pressure on the record company to remove it from the marketplace. In response, the company, Warner, cut out the song from the album that contained it. But Ice-T released later albums on an independent label, further promoting his subversive messages.

Was it really subversive? Did it induce young people to actually murder cops? There is absolutely no evidence that it did. As mentioned, rap's power lay in its ingenious musical treatment of social issues. This caught the attention of everyone, not just teenagers. As it turns out, rap had achieved its tacit goal of awareness-raising by the early 1990s. Having accomplished that, it turned more and more to explicit sexual content for a while. That caused only a minimal stir from the usual suspects (social conservatives). Perhaps most of America had gotten used to youth cultures expressing sexuality in public ways—indeed many of the adults were ex-counterculture and ex-punk members. However, this sexualization of the music was a sign that rap was starting to lose its relevance as a social movement, as its original strident voice became less and less political and discordant. It also started venturing into more lyrical and romantic domains. A new style of rap thus emerged as a broad musical trend throughout the 1990s and early 2000s with artists and bands such as Body Count and Ice-T himself using a new and docile blend of rap, lyricism, and rock that attracted larger audiences.

RAP

The terms *rap* and *hip-hop* started being used interchangeably already in the 1980s. But the former refers more to the musical style itself, whereas the latter designates the attendant lifestyle that the music entails. The movement's early ethos, attitude, historical precedents, and overall worldview are encapsulated in the Sugarhill Gang's marvelous rap classic "Rapper's Delight," which links itself to past youth movements and musical styles, such as rock, counterculture rock, boogie woogie, and the country music of the past.

The subversion subtext in the song is not blatant; it is implicit in the song's modification of English orthography and grammar long before the age of text messages. This was a symbolic critique of the rules of English established by the white mainstream that were easily associated with the same mentality that had enslaved the blacks. Grammar is power; divesting it of this power can be enormously cathartic for subjugated people. The song's homage to the past is seen in allusions to "hip," "hippie," "I gotta bang bang the boogie to the boogie," and "let's rock, you don't stop." Its promotion of a sexually nonchalant attitude is evident in phraseology such as "I'm the C-A-S-an-the-O-V-A," "the rest is F-L-Y." Its encouragement of a new extravagant urban, late-night-clubbish and braggadocio lifestyle is noticeable in expressions such as "I got more clothes than Muhammad Ali," "I dress so viciously I got bodyguards," "I got two big cars," and "I got a Lincoln Continental and a sunroof Cadillac." And its plea that rap is for everyone, not just African Americans, is evident in "see I am Wonder Mike and I'd like to say hello to the black, to the white, the red, and the brown, the purple and yellow." The song suggests, overall, that African Americans can turn their awful plight into one of "delight" by adopting a *carpe diem* lifestyle that is carefree, seizing the pleasures of the moment without thought for the future, and by appealing aesthetically to everyone, not just other African Americans. Of particular interest in the lyrics is the use of "hip" and "hop." As discussed previously, the words *hip* and *hop* have been around since at least the 1920s to describe various styles in African American music. In that era, "Lindy hop" dancing, also known as "jitterbug," became highly popular in Harlem and other parts of black America. The word was also used to describe 1950s rock and roll dancing, as evidenced by Danny and the Juniors in their 1958 hit "At the Hop." The fusion of the two into one, "hip-hop," is suggested by the song as well, thus linking the rap movement to black history and to previous youth trends in music.

Before "Rapper's Delight," the music was seen as inward-looking, a New York style that appealed mainly to break-dancing teens of that city. The song changed that once and for all. Although it faded quickly from the limelight, it managed to attract nationwide interest. In a phrase, if there is one song that turned rap into a new genre that went beyond the New York City perimeter, it was probably this one. The charismatic rapper MC took rap to national TV, showing all America that it was no simple passing fad of inner-city black youths. Shortly thereafter, Kurtis Blow's single "The Breaks," became an unexpected gold record, and a year after that Blondie recorded "Rapture," which became a number-one single across America.

In the national spotlight, rap couldn't help but generate controversy. Body Count's "Cop Killer," as mentioned, evoked moral panic and general indignation; however, this did not last very long. The lyrics were not taken seriously by most rap fans. Like the fans of punk, they understood the theatrical aspects of the music and enjoyed them as such, even though they did allude to injustices in the world. In 1983, Run-D.M.C. came onto the scene, adding evocative rhymes and catchy beats to the basic rap musical template. The style was more "groovy," becoming attractive to youths of all races and social backgrounds. There was also irony and satire in many of the new songs. "Too Short," for example, farcically depicted pimping culture as a parody of ghetto life and its many socio-political ramifications. Rap then got its first video on MTV—Run-D.M.C.'s "Rock Box." A new cadre of rappers with a social conscience emerged. They used the music as a vehicle to talk directly to those underprivileged black youths who put themselves at risk through drug consumption. An example was Melle Mel's release of the anti-cocaine anthem "White Lines." At the same time rap started expanding and diversifying its style blending with other styles, such as jazz, as exemplified by the hit "Rockit" by Herbie Hancock. It took a romantic turn in 1984 with the music of LL Cool J, arguably rap's first heartthrob artist. The first rap-only radio station went on the air that year, KDAY-AM in Los Angeles, and Russell Simmons and Rick Rubin started Def Jam Records, which pushed rap a little closer into the musical mainstream. Women rappers entered the scene in full force in 1985 when Salt-N-Pepa made sexual relations a topic of debate with their hard-hitting lyrics. In the same year 2 Live Crew took sexuality to a new erotic level, eventually getting into legal trouble because of it.

Up to that point, rap had remained primarily a voice—and a powerful one at that—of, by, and for black youths. But in 1986, exactly three decades after Elvis introduced rock and roll to the world in 1956, rap merged with rock to become a powerful new voice for all disenfranchised youths, no matter what their age, background, or race. It was a momentous event, acknowledging the crucial role of African Americans in the constitution of American musical art and the role of young people of the past in bringing about real social change through music. The result was exciting, hip, beautiful, and raucous at once.

HIP-HOP

For many young urban African Americans, hip-hop (the life-style associated with rap) constituted an emotionally powerful social code. The etymological story behind the term *hip-hop* is vague and sounds more like a convenient urban legend than fact. It goes somewhat like this. It was a rapper with Grandmaster Flash and the Furious Five, named Keith Cowboy, who coined the term *hip-hop* at a time when the music was just starting to come into its own and was called simply *rap* (or *disco rap*). He did so in imitation of the rhythmic cadence of marching soldiers. But the connection between marching and rap music is unclear. As discussed before, there is a long history of African Americans' utilization of both terms, *hip* and *hop*.[1] And, as pointed out above, it is more plausible to assume that the term in its hyphen-ated form comes out of the lyrics of "Rapper's Delight," which allude to "hip hop" style as an historical amalgam. The song also insightfully suggests that the difference between hip-hop and past trends is to be found primarily in the "beat."

Among the salient features of the hip-hop code, one that stands out clearly is the requirement to construct a new identity, separate from the one gained through upbringing. This includes the coinage of a new name. By changing one's name to, say, Snoop Dogg, the rap artist takes on, usually in jest, the persona suggested by the name—a "dog" (male) who "snoops" (noses or sniffs around). The sexual joke is obvious.

The new name was called a tag; it was much more than a pseudonym or a nickname. It was a kind of "password" for gain-ing admission into the hip-hop tribe. Hip-hoppers also etched their tags on the urban landscape—on public shelters, buses, subways, signs, walls, freeway overpasses, mailboxes, etc.—with markers, spray paint, or shoe polish. Through this practice they were attempting to symbolically take back the streets.[2] For most hip-hoppers, the streets were their habitat. Hip-hop culture was at first a genuine street culture, as can be seen in early videos, which focused on the street (called "the 'hood"), its dynamics, its narrative potential, and its perils. The tags tell a silent history of "the 'hood." As Rahn suggests, it allowed young blacks to take back the streets to which they belonged.[3] Street life, as Geneva Smitherman also points out, connotes attitudes of "rebelliousness against societal constraints" and the "fierce determination to live on one's own terms."[4]

The early hip-hop documentary *Style Wars* (1983) showed a hilarious scene of tag artists interacting with art-world connoisseurs at a gallery opening, thus juxtaposing art with tagging. In December of 2000, the Brooklyn Museum of Art organized an exposition of 400 pieces of urban street art, called *Hip-Hop Nation: Roots, Rhymes & Rage*, reflecting several decades of tagging art. In a city where nearly 2000 arrests for graffiti offenses were executed in that same year, the art gallery had taken on the role previously confined solely to the streets—legitimizing the art of urban street youths. It was evidence that hip-hop had started to make inroads into general groupthink, despite efforts to suppress it. As this happened, an old nemesis of youth trends started rearing its head. The business world caught on, sensing in the hip-hop lifestyle a social dynamism that was spreading broadly. So, it coopted hip-hop, thereby divesting it of its original subversive or coded meanings. Even high-end fashion brands like Louis Vuitton, Chanel, and Gucci used hip-hop tagging style in their limited edition handbags. The style had migrated everywhere, from clothing fashions to poster design. This was a sure death knell for the movement. Although there were other factors in hip-hop's gradual fade-out by the 2000s, certainly cooption was a major one.

Rap artists all have tags, from LL Cool J, Sister (or Sista) Souljah, and Jay-Z to Snoop Dogg, Busta Rhymes, Lil Jon, Puff Daddy, and Missy Elliot, to mention just a handful. These names are imbued with subtexts, from an obvious facetious sexual one in Snoop Dogg to a descriptive one in Lil Jon. There seems to be an inherent belief in the psychological and social power of the names. This is why hip-hop artists spell their performance names differently—*Dogg* instead of *Dog*, *Sista* instead of *Sister*, and so on. This is an implicit rejection of the rules of language imposed on them by slave masters of the past. So, changing the rules is a sign of liberation. But this practice is not an invention of hip-hop youths. In actual fact, it was present in previous forms of youth culture. In 1952, the African American musician Lloyd Price spelled his hit song "Lawdy Miss Clawdy," in obvious imitation of African American English pronunciation.

Poverty and urban decay in places like the south Bronx produced, as Marcus Reeves puts it, "an environment that had become comparable to the one in 'Lord of the Flies,' where children stranded on an island with no adult guidance create a new, brutal social order of their own."[5] Analogously, hip-hop culture was a Lord-of-the-Flies space that allowed African Americans to create their own type of brutal social order. Defiance is imprinted in hip-hop language. Phrases such as *BIB* or *boyz in blue* (police), *off the hook* (great), and *government cheese* (welfare) are cheeky descriptors of how black youths perceived certain people, institutions, and ideas in white culture. Hip-hop's linguistic style allowed users to intentionally set themselves apart from standard English users through various twists of phrase, spelling creations, and subtle changes in the grammar. This made hip-hop language an anti-hegemonic code.

But the language, like the movement itself, was a blend of reality and fiction. It bespoke of reality because it documented the inner feelings of African Americans perfectly; it was fiction because, as the hip-hoppers themselves sagaciously understood, it did not catch on broadly as a substitute for American English. It was, in the end, a linguistic response to joblessness, poverty, and disempowerment, thus creating an imaginary sense of order through words. It was a form of "resistance discourse"—a way of inveighing indirectly against white America's history of racism and domination. It privileged the urban black street experience and placed the experiences and participation of whites on the periphery of their perspective. This is why white hip-hoppers, like Eminem, used hip-hop language to negotiate their place in the black culture and why many saw him initially as an intruder at worst or a "wannabe" at best.

Hip-hop language is also known as "urban slang." As writer Ruth Cullen observes, when the slang migrates to the suburbs it evanesces there:

> Urban slang—a catchall for hip-hop slang and word on the street—changes at lightning speed. As soon as fast-talking rap artists bend language to suit their rhymes, an array of new media stands poised to share it with the world. Unfortunately, by the time these hip new words and patterns trickle down to the suburbs, they're history. Yesterday's news. Out. Straight up.[6]

Linguist Samy Alim characterizes the slang, instead, as a distinct language—"Hip-hop Nation Language" (HHNL).[7] Alim may be right, since hip-hop also involved refashioning the semantic system of its source language, English, a sure sign that it was declaring its independence from it, in an analogous way, incidentally, to how American English declared its own independence from British English. The controversial word *slut* for "girlfriend" is an example of how hip-hoppers used English with ironically reversed semantics. Along with *ho* and *pimp* to describe a girlfriend and boyfriend respectively, *slut* was used in complimentary, rather than derogatory ways, to designate an attractive female. It was a perfect put-on. Nate Dogg describes his search for a "big old slut" in the single "Shake That"; in the Broadway musical *Avenue Q*, an ample-bosomed puppet is named Lucy the Slut; shops and websites anchored in hip-hop culture promoted a brand of cosmetics called *Slut*; and so on. Significantly, the words *slut* and *ho* were not simply part of male HHNL; they were used by hip-hop women as well as symbols of empowerment, implying that they could put on a "slutty appearance" without reprobation, donning all the trappings of promiscuity without actually being promiscuous. Despite all the warnings of so-called social experts and moral guardians that this sent the wrong messages—the same types of warnings expressed against the flappers in the Roaring Twenties, by the way—no one was listening, outside of the pulpit and a specific part of the polity. The trend, however, quickly passed. Once a put-on or joke gets the laughter it seeks, it loses its effect. So, too, did *slut* and *ho*. They were single-word jokes; and the joke was on white America.

Overall, as linguist Connie Eble aptly puts it, language of this type is "vocabulary with attitude."[8] And, as sociolinguist Bernard Spolsky observes, it is "a kind of jargon marked by its rejection of formal rules, its comparative freshness, its common ephemerality, and its marked use to claim solidarity."[9] It should be mentioned that long before hip-hop talk, similar tendencies were noticeable in youth slang. Young people in the 1920s spelled *rats* as *Rhatz* and shortened "that's too bad" to "stoo bad." Similarly, counterculture youths spelled *tough* as *tuff*, intentionally called themselves *freeks* (spelled that way), and considered their mock spelling of *Amerika* to be a political statement. A number of 1970s and 1980s rock groups spelled their names phonetically rather than with correct orthography. Examples were Guns N' Roses, Led Zeppelin, and the Monkees. Current spelling oddities in urban slang are really manifestations of a transgressive tendency that seems to have always existed within youth culture.

In a way, HHNL was a reflex of an inherent "American rebel" instinct—an instinct that cuts across races and subcultures. Many of the actual features of HHNL are similar or analogous to the ones proposed in the past. For instance, Noah Webster wanted to eliminate the *u* in words such as *colour, harbour, favour,* and *odour* in 1828 because it was not pronounced. His proposal was accepted broadly, becoming one of the features that distinguishes American from British English and thus, by implication, America from its British past. American English is, itself, a language once considered to be subversive by the British themselves (not the King's or Queen's English). As Vivian Cook has perceptively remarked,

> Our discussions of spelling often suggest that there is an ideal of perfect spelling that people should strive for. Correct spelling and punctuation are seen as injunctions carved on tablets of stone; to break them is to transgress the tacit commandments for civilized behaviour. Spelling and punctuation can become an emotional rather than rational area of dispute.[10]

Critics of hip-hop claimed that words such as *slut* may have had a specific semantic intent, but that did not change the fact that they reverberated with a hidden double standard, suggesting ultimately that females existed to be of service to males as sexual entertainers and pleasers. HHNL words like *hump* and *lumps* for the female buttocks and breasts respectively are found throughout early rap lyrics, as if they were objects of desire and defining ones of womanhood itself. Men, on the other hand, are depicted typically as endowed with unique sexual prowess, as *playas*. But the hip-hop women answered the men effectively, demystifying the concept of the sexually endowed "playa" and his purported desirability to women, no matter what their status in life. The women also attacked the view that the male should be free to have his sexual flings with no consequences. In "Me, Myself, and I," Beyoncé decried the hypocrisy of this double standard, suggesting that women are better off by themselves, without their "playa" boyfriends.

The whole "sexual prowess thing" has been interpreted differentially. Some would argue that it was (is) nothing more than a put-on, a carnivalesque form of male sexual braggadocio. Others argue instead that it constitutes outright misogyny and thus cannot just be shrugged off as sexual theatre. The debate is still an ongoing one, but most of the critique comes from spectators, not participants in the culture. This whole line of argument would require much more space than can be accorded to it here. For the present purposes, suffice it to say that, fake or real, one cannot just be an armchair critic in this case. The women themselves are the ones who have the right to answer the supposed misogyny. And they have, quite effectively. Actually, as we have seen, throughout the history of youth culture, female voices have always been prominent ones in bringing out the idiocy of the double standard and the need to rectify the macho mythology behind it. From the flappers to Madonna, the Spice Girls, Beyoncé, and beyond, youth culture has consistently provided a platform for female voices to articulate their own particular slant on sex, romance, and love relations. In a basically patriarchal world, only on the stage of youth theatre could this have occurred with such effectiveness. The audiences listened, allowing women to challenge the stereotypical views of what constitutes female sexuality. Hip-hop and previous youth cultures have made this possible by bringing sex and its myths out in the open, front and centre, for everyone to grasp and debate.

The foregoing discussion does not imply, in any way, that a heightened sense of "hyper-masculinity," as it can be called, is not a factor within hip-hop. After all, most of the early rap musicians were macho males who performed on stage in suggestive sexual ways in order to gain sexual favour from female audiences. Hip-hop is no more macho than any previous form of youth culture. As in all previous attacks on youth trends, sexuality in hip-hop culture has been greatly exaggerated by the mainstream for its own purposes. As Gwendolyn D. Pough points out,

> Hip-Hop may be a uniquely testosterone-filled space, but to say that women have not contributed significantly to its development is false. Women have always been a part of Hip Hop culture and a significant part of rap music.[11]

Just like it was for jazz in a previous era, where males ran the show initially but were joined by females later (many of whom surpassed their male peers in artistry), it is difficult to ignore the massive increase in record deals and sales for women rappers following Salt-N-Pepa's double platinum (2 million) 1986 debut album *Hot, Cool & Vicious*. Since then, female rappers have gained international recognition. As in the past, hip-hop females have been provided with a musical framework through which they can be proud of, and indeed even flaunt, their sexuality. Intersections of sex, race, class, and gender inform, and have always informed, any meaningful reading of youth culture. The lyrics and rhythms of female rappers evoke black female empowerment, making clear their self-identification as African American women. For example, Queen Latifah's Arabic name means "feminine, delicate and gentle." Her role as the Queen Mother of rap was etched in her single "Ladies First" (1989), the first true political commentary rap song by a female artist.[12] Latifah opened the door for Sister Souljah, a former associate of Public Enemy. Souljah's fame grew after her controversial speech at Reverend Jesse Jackson's Rainbow Coalition Leadership Summit in 1992.

There is also considerable diversity in female hip-hop culture. The Queen Mother persona was just one such persona; others included the "Fly Girl," the "Sista with Attitude," and

Photo 5.3: Queen Latifah

Source: MediaPunch Inc / Alamy Stock Photo

the "Black Lesbian." The Fly Girl was someone who dressed in very chic clothing, consisting of miniskirts, sequined fabric, high-heeled shoes, and smart hairstyles, jewellery, and cosmetics. This persona was represented by artists such as Sha Rock of Funky 4 + 1, the Sequence, and the soloist Lady B. The stage and video acts emphasized the female sexual persona, as had Madonna, with its voluptuous curves. The Fly Girl act was vibrant, exciting, and highly empowering. The Sista with Attitude also exuded gender empowerment. As Cheryl Keyes has observed, the Sista with Attitude portrayed herself as an aggressive woman who challenged male authority:

> The Sista with Attitude revises the standard definition of "bitch" to mean an aggressive or assertive female who subverts patriarchal rule. Lyndah of BWP explains, "We use 'Bytches' [to mean] a strong, positive, aggressive woman who goes after what she wants. We take that on today and use it in a positive sense."[13]

The Black Lesbian emerged somewhat from the closet during the 1990s. For example, the artist Queen Pen was probably the first black female artist to openly discuss her lesbianism. Interestingly, Kanye West and others have joined the female's call for a change in male attitudes. Defining manhood by victimizing women is a mindset that must change once and for all in rap culture and in the general society.

GANGSTA CULTURE

The album *Straight Outta Compton* was released in 1988 by the rap group NWA. Songs from the album generated an extraordinary amount of controversy for their violent lyrics, igniting protests from a number of organizations, including the FBI. Lines such as "When I'm called off, I got a sawed off/Squeeze the trigger, and bodies are hauled off" constitute rough, edgy, scary stuff. It was called "gangsta" rap, a hip-hop linguistic rendition of *gangster*. Attempts to censor gangsta rap only served to publicize the music more widely, and, thus, to make it even more attractive to young urban youths generally. The "in your face" street-gang attitude noticeable in gangsta videos, some of which appear to be little more than intimidation displays, was highly worrisome to many at the same time that it was very attractive to many black youths of the era.

It is relevant to note that much has changed since the release of the album. Indeed, even a nostalgic movie based on it was put out in 2015, depicting the career of NWA and the importance of the album both to the history of rap and to the civil rights movement. This was truly a remarkable event, showing how much, purportedly, America had changed. But at another level, the very fact that the movie was made and praised by whites and blacks alike showed that the hip-hop movement had indeed receded to the sidelines. It had lost its political clout, becoming more a part of a historical archive of the civil rights movement than a vibrant and ongoing movement.

In line with the street culture nature of hip-hop generally and the criminal toughness of its ritual code, gangsta rap emerged to add a hard and biting edge to hip-hop—a movement that was, as early as 1988, becoming way too tame and acceptable to many young blacks. The term *gangsta* was perfect, since a gang is really a specific kind of subculture, complete with its own symbolism, language, and *esprit de corps*.

The language used by gangsta rappers was much harsher and more violent than that of previous rappers. It was similar to the criminal's cant, a code intended for use by gang insiders only. Gangsta rap reflected the every-man-for-himself struggle of the ghetto, not a politics of solidarity. It was both a reflection on the history of racism and a call to arms to change the situation. Reactions to gangsta rap within hip-hop culture itself were mixed. A politically savvy activist, Sister Souljah claimed that only women have the mettle to really change things in her "360 Degrees," not the alpha males. Perhaps sensing the failure of ersatz military movements, Sister Souljah came to realize that the musical pen was indeed mightier than the gun. As she puts it in her song, men have always chosen the path of the gun and failed miserably. It is now up to African American women to change things, because they have the real "chemistry" for bringing about change, a chemistry, to paraphrase Sister Souljah, consisting of aesthetic thoughts that flow endlessly.

Actually, predating *Straight Outta Compton* is Ice-T's 1986 song "6 in the Mornin'," which is seen as the prototype, since it was all about guns, beating people up, and other acts of violence that mirrored what was happening on the real streets. The music was basically rap, but it introduced a hard-driving style, evocative of metal and punk at their most acerbic and aggressive. Gangsta rap soon spawned its own subgenres, such as Mafioso rap, which flourished in the 1990s, as an extension of so-called East Coast rap, itself a declared adversary and bitter foe of West Coast rap. Indeed, the gangsta rappers taunted and challenged each other in their songs, bringing about actual duels and confrontations in real life.

Not all black artists and intellectuals took to the gangsta message, or to its constant pummeling out of themes that seemed to stigmatize blacks rather than liberate them from their past—profanity, violence, promiscuity, misogyny, street gangs, vandalism, drive-by shootings, drug dealing, and blatant sexism. Spike Lee, for example, criticized it astringently in his satirical film *Bamboozled* (2000) as being nothing more than a modern day "black minstrel show" in which the characters acted and talked in the stereotypical fashion expected of blacks. The overall picture that emerges from the gangsta lifestyle, Lee suggests, was a big step backwards, not forward, as Sister Souljah also implied. Gangsta life is caricaturization, not transformation and empowerment. The gangsta movement was, thus, a symptom of the African American's struggle both within and without—"Do I rebel and forge my own identity or do I comply and work within the system?" Spike Lee's movie brings out this inner tension perfectly, suggesting that the only resolution is evolutionary. The election of Barack Obama seemed, for a while, to have tilted the scales in Spike Lee's favour. However, this seems to have changed in 2016, as mentioned briefly at the start of this chapter.

In his 1984 single "Gangster Boogie," Schoolly D tells of how he put his pistol against another rapper's head in order to instill fear in him. Toughness, fear-mongering, control of the streets, and intimidation became the themes around which gangsta rap revolved. But gangsta did not last—its fade-away came when the genre started to assume a more melodious and flexible musical style. This was because of its commercial success and its spread. Attempts to redefine the boundary line between mainstream rap and gangsta rap by artists such as MIMS and Soulja Boy were largely unsuccessful. The world of the new millennium was a very different one than that of the 1980s and 1990s. The gangsta movement simply fizzled out, perhaps because the Internet gave black youth a new tool to communicate their messages of dissent and thus to enter into the world of "penmanship," where the tools of literacy are more powerful than the sword, as Sister Souljah had implied in her 1992 song.

As mentioned above, Reeves characterized the whole rap movement as a "Lord-of-the-Flies" one which had special appeal to dispossessed street youth.[14] The 1954 novel *Lord of the Flies*, by William Golding, came, in fact, at about the same time that youth gangs were coming into their own in large urban cores. Based on Golding's wartime experiences, it explores moral dilemmas and human reactions in extreme situations. Gangsta culture is a product of these reactions. Golding's novel also contains an important subtext—the quest for order is what drives human beings. The novel tells of a group of schoolboys stranded on an uninhabited island after an airplane crash that kills all the adults on the plane. Only the youths survived. They had been taken away from England because of a nuclear war. The boys try to create their own society but gradually lose their moral compass and develop savage ways of behaving and interacting, including primitive sacrificial rites and murder. They try to save themselves through planning—a renewal of civilized behaviour. They divide themselves into hunters (doers) and fire-keepers (thinkers). But the two groups soon begin to fight. The boys are eventually rescued and returned home.

The points of comparison between gangsta lifestyle and the novel are transparent. As in the novel, the original gangstas were "returned home." The sign that this happened was the movie *Bamboozled* as mentioned above. The movie made it obvious as well that gangsta culture had, overall, been of benefit, not only to African American youths, but also to society in general, which has since come to reflect much more cogently upon the treatment of blacks. The anger inherent in gangsta rap is a deep abiding one. It may have given youth black culture a black eye in some people's minds, but its overall message caused a stir and may have even led to radical attitude shifts in America at large. As rap faded in the early 2000s, its outlaw image morphed into one that was not unlike the image of disco culture—better to dance the night away than to engage in drive-by shootings. In retrospect, it might have been a form of therapy for young black Americans, allowing them to come to grips with their hopeless lives, much like Holden Caulfield did on a psychologist's couch. By speaking about his angst, Holden had to come to grips with it; by rapping about their particular kind of angst, black youths were probably trying to come to grips with it too.

EPILOGUE

From 1987 to 1989, rap started to diversify noticeably, mixing in elements of politics, sex, and romance, along with musical snippets from the past. DJ Jazzy Jeff and the Fresh Prince, additionally, injected prurient comedy routines into rap, and four "rap hippies" called De La Soul added parody and goofiness to the genre by toting daisies as part of their persona. At the same time, Public Enemy continued the tradition of using explicit political messages in their lyrics. Rap, like rock and roll, had developed a split personality—the sure sign that it was about to fade. Cooption and entry into the mainstream, by the late 1990s, made it ripe for disintegration. By the start of the new millennium, rap had morphed from *the* voice of youth culture to many fragmented voices.

By the end of the 1990s, Jay-Z had sanitized rap into a general musical genre for large audiences. In 1997, Puff Daddy, Wyclef Jean, and Missy Elliott also made rap popular with all age groups by rendering it musically and lyrically more generic. In 1998, Big Pun, Lauryn Hill, and Ja Rule turned rap into a multi-layered spectacle of song and dance. In other words, by the end of the 1990s, rap's voice started to have less and less of a subversive and raucous tone to it. It had become big business. Kanye West, for example, became one of the most successful producers in music history. And, in 2004, Tupac Shakur posthumously surpassed 37 million in total album sales, which ranked him among the top 40 pop artists of all time.

It was inevitable that rap would fade into the background. It had spoken, loudly and clearly, throughout the 1980s and 1990s. Its message at the millennium was not as monolithic. And although it is still around, and some (perhaps many) still see themselves as rappers, the "walk" is not as powerful as it was in 1986. Rap now shares the limelight with other styles and voices, including those who continue on with their neo-hippie,

Photo 5.4: Tupac Shakur

Source: ZUMA Press, Inc. / Alamy Stock Photo

neo-punk, and neo-anything lifestyles. The motivation for the hip-hop movement, encapsulated in the late Tupac Shakur's marvelous song "Changes" is a faint one. Tupac was murdered at the age of 25 by unknown assailants. He grew up in the ghettos of New York and later moved to Los Angeles where he spent the rest of his short life, which became a paradigm for young black Americans. He spent time in prison, was acquitted for the shooting of a police officer, was shot five times himself, and left the world some of the most moving music ever written.

With "Changes," Tupac emphasized the need for change to occur not only in his own life but also in black communities. With lines such as "Tired of being poor and even worse I'm black, my stomach hurts so I'm looking for a purse to snatch," Tupac encapsulated the tragedy of the situation facing many blacks. When basic survival needs such as food become unattainable, antisocial behaviours surface. Tupac suggested that there was a conspiracy from the higher echelons of mainstream white society to make sure that black communities had access to guns and drugs so that they could destroy themselves: "First ship them dope and let them deal the brothas, give them guns step back and watch them kill each other." It is hard to ignore Tupac's message to this day.

The rise of rap parallels in many ways the birth of rock and roll. Both originated in African American culture and both were initially aimed at black audiences. In both, the new style gradually attracted white musicians, who made it popular to white audiences. For rock and roll the musician was Elvis Presley; for rap it was Aerosmith. And like rock and roll, rap became more and more soft, obeying a kind of inherent musical law of regression, with the mean being melody and harmony. In the mid-1990s, rap had started to regress toward the mean.

A *New York Times* 2002 survey found that most of the top rap artists at the time were already "historical figures." The *Times* rappers included Dr. Dre, Warren G, Puff Daddy,

Shaggy, DMX, Nelly, Ludacris, Coolio, Snoop Dogg, and duo Salt-N-Pepa. A *Rolling Stone* poll taken in the same year asked its readers to choose their all-time favorite albums. *Revolver* by the Beatles (1965) turned out to be the number one of all time; *Nevermind* by Nirvana (1991) and *Appetite for Destruction* (1987) by Guns N' Roses were also in the top 10 list, which did not contain a single rap album. Although the age demographic of *Rolling Stone*'s readership was an upward one at the time, it is nevertheless surprising to find that rap had faded away, not leaving any legacy beyond its racial perimeter. Perhaps the old spectre of predictability and familiarity entered into the picture. Once some musical style becomes popular and predictable it tends to fade.

With its own magazines, movies, radio stations, television programs, websites, footwear, clothing, alcohol beverages, and jewelry, the rap movement had also become big business by the early 2000s—another sign of demise. P. Diddy (Puff Daddy) was the owner of his own record label (Bad Boy), clothing company (Sean John), and television show (Da Band). His rapping days were basically over. The rap movement had made a lot of rappers rich, leaving most other blacks behind. It was seen by some, therefore, as hypocritical in the end.[15] But this is not correct. The driving force that attracted inner-city ghetto African American youths to rap music was, in fact, its anti-hegemonic attitude and its ability to give expression to socially powerless voices. The focal element was the music. Rapper Chuck D boldly articulated rap's anti-hegemonic stance in a 1992 interview with *XXL* (a popular rap magazine) as follows: "This is our voice, this is the voice of our lifestyle, this is the voice of our people. We're not going to take the cookie cutter they give us to let them mold us."

Today, that voice is hardly powerless. Many young people still listen to rap, and hip-hop has spread somewhat throughout the global village, merging with other styles. One of the best selling albums of 2008 was a rap album, *Tha Carter III*, by Lil Wayne, reviving some interest in the original power of rap as political statement. In the end, rap made a difference. Despite the outcome of the 2016 presidential elections, the voice of America today includes black voices. As Jay-Z stated in the opening epigraph to this chapter, "Hip-hop has done more than any leader, politician, or anyone to improve race relations."[16]

CHAPTER 6

Demise: The Day the Music Died

Science and technology multiply around us. To an increasing
extent they dictate the languages in which we speak and think.
Either we use those languages, or we remain mute.

—*J.G. Ballard (1930–2009)*

PROLOGUE

The new millennium has brought radical changes shaped by an ever-expanding reliance on technology. These include changes in traditional social institutions, in communicative behaviour, and, more to the point of the present book, in our perceptions and experiences of both the coming-of-age period and youth culture generally. The changes are so drastic that they may have finally brought about an end to the generation gap and, thus, to the *raison d'être* of a separate youth culture.

Starting in the mid-2000s, with the arrival of social media, the modern world started taking a hugely different path from any of the paths it had taken in the past—leading to a need to revise all previous conceptualizations of what history is and what culture means in a global context as people of all languages enter into daily contact through the computer screen and other digital devices. The historical flow from one generation to a subsequent one that has characterized youth culture since the 1920s may have finally been interrupted. There are now more "fragments" of previous youth cultures, as witnessed by millennial followers of metal, punk, and hip-hop, than there are new (if any) musical trends that can be seen as descendants of past ones. There also seems to be no sense of anticipation that something "big" musically is about to occur; nor does there seem to be a desire to undertake a Siddhartha-like spiritual journey into the "forest" of reality. People now have a new "forest" at their fingertips. It's called the Internet. In that virtual world the past has become dim and perhaps, to some, irrelevant. Notions such as adolescence and youth culture may be things of that past and thus less relevant today.

Has the historical chain of youth-movement-after-youth-movement that was forged in the 1920s finally been broken? As discussed throughout this book, the key to understanding the history of youth culture is music. Each new musical style spearheaded a youth movement that, in turn, changed the world in some way. But there seems to be no new type of music being developed that can come forward to spearhead new movements—political, social, and cultural. The reason for this may well be technology—which ironically both entrenched youth culture in the past and now may be a main factor in bringing about its demise. Elvis and Green Day now come up on the same sidebar on YouTube. Alongside pop music celebrities, such as Beyoncé, Lady Gaga, and Justin Bieber, one finds retro trends throughout the global village, not to mention indie music scattered throughout cyberspace. One can locate any style or genre of music on the Web and check the playlists of others and popularity ratings on the sites themselves. This may have led overall to what journalist Simon Reynolds calls *retromania*, referring to a vague nostalgia felt by people about the icons and the fads of the past.[1] Current artists themselves seem to be looking back rather than forward.

This is not to say that today's young people have lost the desire to change things and make the world right. The support that millennials showed for Bernie Sanders—an ex-hippie—during the 2016 presidential campaign is concrete evidence that they do care greatly about the state of the world. And, as in the hippie 1960s, protest and a general critique of society still can be found in a variety of musical genres. But there is a difference—music is no longer a unifying force for change. The reason for this may well be that the Internet has given the power to anyone to become a rock star. The randomness and dispersive nature of online musical culture is the greatest impediment of all to adding another link to the youth culture historical chain. And without music there is no youth culture.

Perhaps, in the end, the *raison d'être* of youth culture was a product and consequence of a previous social reality, as discussed in the opening chapter, with its needs and aspirations. The question of whether youth culture, understood as a culture based on music and its derivative lifestyle trends, is coming to an end is a relevant and important one, since it tells us something about ourselves today. The purpose of this chapter is to broach that very question, although in no way will it be possible to answer it conclusively. Indeed, it is virtually impossible to make assertions in an age where change is a daily affair and yesterday's predictions are today's facts.

TECHNOLOGY AND THE MASS MEDIA

The great communications theorist Marshall McLuhan often claimed that culture, social evolution, and technology are so intertwined that we hardly ever realize their dynamic interaction, because it occurs without awareness.[2] We can witness this happening concretely today when a new digital device comes onto the market. In no time, it becomes not just a handy accoutrement: it changes how we live and interact and even how we think. It is worth paraphrasing McLuhan's ideas here since they provide a key to understanding the likely reasons why youth culture may be on the verge of demise.

McLuhan was among the first to realize that changes in mass technologies lead to changes in culture, social structure, language, and knowledge systems, following up on the concepts of his own teacher Harold Innis.[3] Technology, in the McLuhanian paradigm, is any tool, physical or cognitive, that is used to do something old in a new, efficient, and extensive way. Alphabets, which emerged around 1000 BCE, constituted a new technology in this sense, since they allowed for an efficient way to encode and use knowledge, allowing written texts to emerge as pivotal to civilization's progress. Alphabetic writing allows for a small set of symbols to store and use information economically and more permanently than oral transmission. The alphabet, consequently, brought about the first paradigm shift in human cognition and in the world's social structure, a structure that previously depended mainly on orally transmitted knowledge, which is less likely to be stable. Myth is the mode of knowledge in oral cultures; history is the mode in literacy-based cultures. Alphabets constituted the initial step towards the establishment of a worldwide civilization, making print *the* medium for storing and exchanging ideas across the world. After the development of movable type technology, the "print age" emerged, since the technology made it possible to print and duplicate books massively and cheaply. McLuhan called the new world order the "Gutenberg Galaxy," after Johannes Gutenberg, the German printer who invented typographic technology in Europe. The Gutenberg Galaxy established printed books as the primary media for recording and preserving information and knowledge. The consequences of that invention were felt throughout the world. Print literacy encouraged individualism and the growth of nationalism. It brought about the Protestant Reformation, the Enlightenment, and the Romantic Movement. These would have been literally unthinkable in oral societies.

Another paradigm shift occurred in the twentieth century, after advances in technologies established new electronic mass media for communicating information. Since electronic signals can cross borders virtually unimpeded, McLuhan characterized the world that was being united by such media as a "global village." We are now living in that village, a village where youths can congregate via social media, rather than physically in hangout venues of the past. As a result, young people in various parts of the world become deeply involved in the lives of everyone else. Ironically, McLuhan argued, this situation would lead to the end of the print age, and to the growth of new communities that showed the same kinds of characteristics of early tribes. This included less reliance on the validity of history and a new type of mythic thinking based on stories that circulate in cyberspace—similar to the kinds of myths that characterized early cultures.

Particularly relevant is McLuhan's idea that tools (not only in the literal sense of the word but also in his own sense of intellectual artifacts) are extensions or amplifications of sensory, physical, or intellectual faculties or capacities. An axe, for example, extends or amplifies the ability of the human hand to break wood; the wheel the ability of the human foot to cover great distances; and so on. This theory of amplification goes a long way towards explaining the effects of the youth-technology synergy throughout the twentieth century. When radio came onto the scene, young people unconsciously accepted it as an extension of their communal ear, so to speak. What they heard was perceived as involving others, thus instilling a sense of community among the listeners. The consequences were monumental. Because electronic modes of transmission increase the speed at which people can communicate and can reach many more instantly, they have had the effect of altering modes of sensory communication. McLuhan condensed this idea into his now classic phrase "the medium is the message":

> The medium is the message. This is merely to say that the personal and social consequences of any medium—that is, of any extension of ourselves—result from the new scale that is introduced into our affairs by each extension of ourselves, or by any new technology.[4]

There is little doubt that youth culture would not have come into being without the mass media to spread it or, more accurately, to extend it, thus uniting youths everywhere in spirit. Radio was the amplification conduit in the 1920s that allowed any young person to feel part of a community. Television extended this even more so from the 1950s to the millennium. Of course, records, CDs, and other recording objects also helped promote and embed youth trends and, thus, allow movements to perpetuate themselves through broad diffusion. In all this, the attention of the mass media has always been critical. Without such interest, youth trends would have come and gone quickly. In the 1920s, the radio became obsessed with the flappers and with jazz. The mass media had discovered that audiences wanted and desired excitement; jazz provided it. In the 1950s, the media focused on rock and roll, Elvis Presley, sock hops, and rebellion. Television jumped on the bandwagon with newscasts and documentaries about what rock and roll was, or was not, doing to society. At first, religious zealots were seen breaking Elvis's records on TV as an act of repulsion against the "devil's music," as it was called. It didn't matter, though. Young people felt the excitement of his music and his performances. It stirred them on to carve out a lifestyle apart from that of adults.

In the counterculture era, television images of hippies protesting, smoking pot in the open, and attending mass concerts saturated the airwaves. Television brought the hippie movement to everyone's awareness. As the movement became violent, the cameras were there once again with pundits taking sides, for or against the riots and protests. The media in the post-counterculture era, with its fragmented youth subcultures, started to distance itself somewhat from the new trends as such—a sign that these were no longer as interesting, special, or newsworthy, unless they were associated with some scandal or some new lifestyle. Madonna and Michael Jackson, alongside punks, disco scenes, raves, and the like, did catch the media's attention, but the interest seemed to fade more quickly than in previous eras. Perhaps the reason was that there were too many subcultures, making it impossible for one of them to rise above the others to become dominant. Youth culture was no longer unique or different enough from other trends in society to garner any particular attention. The subsequent rap era did catch the media's attention once again, but the mainly white media outlets at the time saw it as something that was specific to African Americans, with some emphasis on the racial implications of the movement.

The rebellion and revolution that previous youth cultures heralded simply seemed to have lost steam by the end of the 1990s, as attention veered towards the implications of the Internet. The youth music-media partnership was becoming less profitable, losing the market potential it once had. Technology was crucial to both the birth and demise of youth culture. The flapper lifestyle of the 1920s would have gone unnoticed beyond a few cities, eliminating the possibility for the development of generalized youth culture movements in subsequent years, if it were not for records and the spread of the new music via the radio. The cheapness and growing availability of mass-produced vinyl records and gramophones (record players) and the advent of radio led to a true paradigm shift in the society of that era—the entrenchment of youth music as a kind of default music. The new technologies helped to embed styles such as jazz and swing beyond the perimeter of youth culture. Young people bought the records and the radio stations played them. Shortly thereafter, many adults jumped in, modifying the new music to suit their own aesthetics. In the mid-1950s, this pattern reached a critical mass, producing the first culture identifiable as "made by adolescents, for adolescents only"—rock and roll culture.

Radio broadcasting in particular was highly influential in establishing this pattern at the start. It brought news, information, and the arts directly into homes. Historically a privilege of the elite, these could now be enjoyed by all members of the public, literate or not, rich or not, given that most would otherwise not have access to venues such as the concert hall and the theatre. The parallel growth of network radio and Hollywood cinema, both of which were launched as massive commercial enterprises in the mid-1920s, created an unprecedented mass culture for people of all social classes and educational backgrounds. The democratization of the arts had started in earnest, and youths were front and centre in this process. In the mid-1950s, the rock and roll experiment would have passed into oblivion had it not been for new record-making technologies, the radio hit parades that promoted the music, and TV programs, such as *American Bandstand*, that showcased the music and its derivative lifestyle throughout the United States. Without those records, hit parades, and TV programs, the tide would have quickly turned, and youth culture might have disappeared as a social force right there and then.

The gist of the foregoing discussion is that youth culture and the mass media had, up to and including the counterculture era, forged a partnership that benefited ratings on one side (the media) and allowed social empowerment on the other (youth culture). The medium was truly the message in this case. As the media started focusing less and less on youth trends as significant, and as the trends themselves became habitual and even predictable, the game was starting to come to an end. By the turn of the millennium, the mass media had lost interest in youth movements (if there were any), focusing instead on the ways millennials used the new technologies and what these meant socially and psychologically in the global village. Adolescence itself as a psychological category seemed to have faded, as children started using computers and social media at earlier ages thus rendering the supposed trauma of adolescence irrelevant. As the world changed through technology, youth culture has lost its *raison d'être*. In a world of nano-celebrities, memes, and viral videos, there is no social substratum from which a powerful new youth movement can emerge. Everything has a short shelf life. There are popular singers and momentary trends, but the social environment for these to spread and coalesce into a veritable movement is not there in the global village.

Another sure sign that youth culture as a distinct entity has started to wane is the fact that new trends do not stir moral panic, at least in the way that previous trends did. The ephemerality of a trend, now called a "meme," guarantees that this will not foment and become sustainable. People of all ages are exposed to the same memes, at the same time, in a virtual way. We are now all part of a "meme simulacrum." What is behind the screen is as important as, if not more than, what is on this side of it (the real world), but in a very ephemeral way. The irony is that older people are no longer shocked about new trends in the way that older people were in previous eras. Age-based preferences are becoming a thing of the past, as people of every age engage in the same kinds of trends on and off the screen.

Moral panic theory was proposed initially by Stan Cohen in his insightful study of "mods" and "rockers."[5] Whether it was alarmed reactions to Elvis's swinging pelvis or to the bizarre and gross antics on stage of punk rockers, moral panic was always evoked by trends among adolescents or shifts in youth culture. This in itself provided evidence that youths were indeed making an impact on the mainstream, that is, by provoking a reaction of sorts. Of course, transgressive trends gradually lost their impact, blending silently and seamlessly into the larger cultural mainstream or disappearing altogether, as the makers and followers of those trends became older. So, the moral panic expressed by adults at certain periods was temporary and generation-specific. Nevertheless, it was a sign that youth movements mattered in a kind of reverse-psychology way. Right up to gangsta culture, moral panic was seemingly a constant in society. The fact that new trends that seem bizarre or even subversive now garner little attention, let alone condemnation, is an indirect sign of demise. Indifference is a sign of irrelevance.

Because of technology, youth culture has become less and less tied to adolescence. Youth is no longer the privilege of the young. Due to an increase in average life expectancy and a raising of affluence levels (when compared to previous historical periods), the prospect of living longer, and having more money at one's disposal, makes it possible to engage in trends once considered to be solely "teen stuff." The result is an effacement of the traditional line between "young" and "old." Youth has, in effect, become a collective state of mind. This does not mean that young people are not interested in justice, civil rights, and bringing wars to an end as were their predecessors. They are. But they do not need new styles of music or clothing, or whatever else was used in the past. They have a new way of initiating protests—social media. Moral panic cannot gain any momentum in this new virtual world. If it does emerge, it literally has itself the lifespan of a meme or a viral video.

CYBERSPACE

To summarize the foregoing argument, cyberspace may have eliminated the generation gaps and moral panics of the past. It is an environment that has made these things based in nostalgia. Youth culture was a product of the Post-Industrial age; that age has gone, taking youth culture along with it. We are now in an "information age" that is resistant and indifferent to the formation of sustainable aesthetic trends. And it has truly rendered the psychological theory of adolescence, which has existed since the latter part of the nineteenth century, virtually irrelevant. Even childhood is no longer what it was once purported to be—a magical world of the imagination located in Neverland. Children in war-torn countries are trained to be warriors, not to look for fairies or adventure in Neverland. Children are trained to use computers and navigate the Internet as soon as it is cognitively possible to do so. Gone is the magical power of Fantasyland. It is for children and adults equally today. With diminishing myths to sustain childhood, its "natural" progression into adolescence is being questioned more and more. G. Stanley Hall's book (Chapter 1) is now read as a curious historical document, not as the predecessor to understanding the psychology of adolescence. Freud and his descendants have also started receding into the background.

Cyberspace is the term coined by American novelist William Gibson in his 1984 novel *Neuromancer*, a novel that was the inspiration for modern-day science fiction narratives, which typically take place in a bleak, dehumanized future society dominated by technology and robotic humans. Gibson's description of cyberspace is worth repeating here:

> Cyberspace. A consensual hallucination experienced daily by millions of legitimate operators. A graphic representation of data abstracted from the banks of every computer in the human system. Unthinkable complexity. Lines of light ranged in the nonspace of the mind, clusters of constellations of data. Like city lights, receding.[6]

Life in cyberspace has its own set of rules, quite unlike those of real space. It creates a "consensual hallucination," as Gibson put it, or to use Jean Baudrillard's term, a "simulacrum," whereby the hyperreal world of the screen is where we now live on a daily basis; it has become a counterpart and often a substitute for the real space in which our bodies exist.[7] As urban scientist Michael Benedikt notes, in cyberspace "the tablet becomes a page becomes a screen becomes a world, a virtual world. Everywhere and nowhere, a place where nothing is forgotten yet everything changes."[8] Our Facebook pages and our tweets define us, remaining in cyberspace even beyond our physical lives. This is affecting not only how we live but also how we view mortality. Cyberspace is strangely uniting us at the same time that it is making personal choice and activity important. This might explain why youth culture, if it even exists, has little relevance in hyperreality.

A new way of congregating, or organizing encounters, has crystallized because of cyberspace. It is the new hangout. Gone are the diners of the 1950s, nostalgically revisited by *Happy Days* (Chapter 2). Enter chat rooms, Facebook, Twitter,

Instagram—all virtual hangouts that hardly bring young people together into a veritable community. These do have impacts, of course. They dictate political trends and even influence election outcomes. But they are not conducive to the establishment of a new youth culture. Cyberspace has changed how individuals experience their adolescence by altering the ways in which identity is created and managed.

For most of the twentieth century, young people used technology receptively. That was because of the one-way nature of the technology. Teens listened to radio to receive the new music. They could not click on to their favourite songs on YouTube. Nor could they download anything. They had to go to the local record store and buy the records or CDs they wanted. The tastemakers were, in a sense, the record labels. The only medium that was interactive, or bidirectional, was the telephone. Starting in the 1960s, the phone became a major conduit for permitting interaction among adolescents. But the range of the interaction was limited and local.[9] The main form was of the face-to-face variety in locales such as school, shopping malls, parks, diners, or wherever the neighbourhood hotspot for teens to congregate and hang out was located. When they did communicate with others outside of such physical venues, which was rarely, they wrote letters or made telephone calls. At the turn of the millennium, all this changed. The Internet and mobile devices have come forward to completely revolutionize communication among young people, changing the whole texture of youth interaction itself and eliminating the power of the hangout to unify young people. The Internet allows teens to converse in real time.[10] Text messaging and similar SMS communications have largely replaced phone talk.

Has all this truly changed the nature of adolescence? In a study of South Korean youth, Kyongwon Yoon found that there were three kinds of relationship-maintaining behaviours teens maintained via technology.[11] The first was to connect primarily with those who are a part of their daily lives; for example, to keep in touch with school peers. The second was to maintain relationships with those who were a part of a broader social network, such as friends who attended other schools. The third was to develop and acquire new friendships and to strengthen initial face-to-face encounters. In effect, Yoon concludes, the new technology has allowed young people to interact virtually, rather than physically. The latter is a consequence of the former, and not the other way around. This extends to dating, where relations occur online at times before they do offline.

But there are new troubles emerging in cyberspace that are, arguably, even more conflictual than those before. There is great humiliation in discovering a private photo of oneself posted on the Internet or in finding a website or Facebook page filled with personal information, gossip, and abusive comments directed at some peer. Cyberspace has taken bullying to new heights. The anonymity of online communication gives bullies a new form of power to attack others with little risk of being caught. And because there is no actual physical contact with their victims, their feelings of empathy and remorse are much less pronounced than they would be otherwise.

MEME CULTURE

Perhaps the most significant aspect of cyberspace with regard to the present argument is that it is practically impossible in that hyperreal space for a sustained and thus meaningful youth culture to meld and gain prominence. Cyberspace produces a "meme culture" where trends come forth quickly and disappear just as quickly. Cyberspace is where everything is easily transformed into momentary fads, forms of entertainment, and instantaneous gratifications. This goes contrary to all the technologically supported youth cultures of the past—radio culture, cinema culture, television culture, and so on—which created the conditions for the cultures to materialize and become entrenched. In meme culture, there is little or no stability—trends literally come and go. Everything is becoming subject to the laws of entropy, whereby rapid deterioration is the underlying principle of mechanical and social systems alike. The disruptive chaos that the punks wanted to bring about has been accomplished, ironically, by the Internet.

Meme culture is a pastiche culture whereby anything can be put together within the same space, from advancements in physics to momentary fads in music and humour. This state of affairs has truly transformed the world, blurring the lines between serious culture and entertainment culture. If something is not instant and of brief duration, then it probably will not garner any attention at all, unless we are looking for some specific kind of information. And if it is broadly interesting, then the TED Talk is sufficient to bring its importance out.[12]

This situation has given a significant blow to the possibility of the emergence of a unified and sustained youth culture. Music has always been the fuel behind this culture. Youths would rally around a group (for example, the Beatles), a genre (for example, punk rock), an artist (for example, Elvis Presley), or a musically based lifestyle trend (for example, the flappers). These rallies revolved around records and albums, bought in stores. Possessing an album such as *Sgt. Pepper's Lonely Hearts Club Band* was a momentous event. One literally "carried" the revolution in one's hands by holding the album. Today, anyone can make a playlist of thematically disconnected songs—they are interesting but they hardly constitute elements that undergird a unified movement. The "mashpedia" culture that this has brought about is an antiserum against the possibility of any new unified youth culture emerging. Cyberspace is truly where "the music died."

As semiotician Roland Barthes argued, the constant craving for new things, new spectacles, new fads, new celebrities, and so on, is a state of mind fuelled by capitalism.[13] Obsolescence is, in a consumerist culture, something to be avoided, whether it is the type of television set one has or the mobile digital device one has recently purchased. In the Internet Age, Barthes' view seems to have become a fact as we are bombarded more and more by neo-fads, neo-styles, and neo-celebrities. The Internet has been a powerful democratizing force, giving everyone a voice and a locus for bringing to light new ideas, new artistic forms, and the like. But it has also given a powerful strident voice to faddishness and trendiness. As in all previous eras of human life, there needs to be a balance between the serious and the faddish, the solemn and the comedic.

To see how meme culture inhibits a youth trend from solidifying, consider the Gangnam Style craze—a dance craze introduced by Psy (Park Jae-Sang), a South Korean performer and songwriter known for his comedy performances in Korea. Psy became an international celebrity when, on December 21, 2012, his music video "Gangnam Style" surpassed one billion views on YouTube—the first video ever to do so.

The incredible success of the meme got Psy the opportunity to appear on television programs such as the *Today Show* and *Saturday Night Live* and in concerts such as the Times Square New Year's Eve celebration of 2012, among many others. Pop musicians started following and promoting Psy on social media. He was also signed by a major label, Schoolboy Records. But by early 2014, the Gangnam Style meme had literally dissolved away in cyberspace. Nothing came out of it to rival, for example, the Charleston or the Twist as a lasting style of dancing. As communication theorist Limor Shifman argues, there are now popular meme genres that, as with anything else in Web 2.0 culture, hardly get noticed beyond initial interest.[14]

In 2010, a YouTube video showed a New York band called Atomic Tom playing one of its songs, "Take Me Out," using only iPhones. Over two million people viewed the video. The large audience for a clip such as this one illustrates the larger

Photo 6.1: Psy "Gangnam Style" Dancing

Source: Screenshot from the music video for "Gangnam Style"

phenomenon of the randomness of success. In the past, youth culture movements were evolutionary—previous trends were restructured into new ones—not random occurrences. Jazz went into the formation of swing, boogie-woogie into rock and roll, rock and roll itself into counterculture rock, and so on. This evolutionary flow has been disrupted, perhaps once and for all, by meme culture. Previous youth culture movements can thus be characterized as "genetic"; "memetic" culture has no evolutionary thrust to it and, so, no tributary can spring from it.

ADOLESCENCE REVISED

Recall that it was Erik Erikson (Chapter 1) who first emphasized the importance of identity construction at adolescence. Today, it occurs in cyberspace more than it does elsewhere. This is changing how young people view themselves. And this, in turn, is changing the accepted views of adolescence.

This has brought about new dangers, as some adolescents try to efface their birth identity and "try on" a different identity in a perilous fashion. This was the theme, actually, of a PBS documentary called *Growing Up Online* (January 22, 2008). The filmmakers spoke to a number of teenagers about their online habits. One girl named "Autumn" (which was not her real name) was a 14-year-old who felt that she "never fit the mould" in her New Jersey town and was horribly teased about it as a result. So, she reinvented herself online as Autumn Edows, a sexy model and creative artist. She took scantily clad photos of herself and posted them on her personal blog. She began to enjoy all the attention she was receiving, attracting many new friends through her online persona and garnering hundreds of comments telling her she was beautiful, sexy, and artistic. Autumn was constantly on her computer, and her parents had absolutely no knowledge of her online social life. She herself was somewhat unsure of her new identity, although she did feel empowerment: "I didn't feel like myself, but I liked that I didn't feel like myself." When the school principal discovered her photographs, he labelled them as pornographic. Autumn's mother intervened and forced her daughter to delete every single file. Autumn's popularity disappeared and she fell back into a depressive state. She responded by saying that such intervention devastated her: "If you have something that is that meaningful to you, to have it taken away is like your worst nightmare."

The filmmakers also spoke to a group of girls who, in the fall of 2006, were trading insults on MySpace. They would post comments on their profiles and insult each other for no reason, displaying their conflicts on the site. In physical reality, however, there was no such turbulence, until "they had left a comment on one of their friends' page talking about her," and she blurted out, "You can't say it to my face. I'm right here," which resulted in a brawl. The school principal later reported having seen students videotaping the fight, which was posted on YouTube. Afterwards, the girls reported feeling "famous."

These are indeed worrisome events, suggesting that the models of identity construction of the past may now be irrelevant and, thus, that the whole notion of adolescence needs to be revisited. As we saw in the opening chapter, the construction of adolescence laid the groundwork for youth cultures to emerge, from the flappers to the rappers—youth cultures that reacted to social conditions, of which adolescence itself was one. Setting themselves apart from the adult mainstream, adolescents started forming distinct movements by themselves. Adolescence and youth culture, in the real world, were two sides of the same coin. Neither one came from nature; they both came from historical forces that allowed them to emerge.

This is quite a radical turn in the history of youth culture. There is no new movement around the corner, as far as can be seen. The Beatles may have known intuitively all along that such a time would come to pass. In their marvellous song "Across the Universe," they described poetically how the "words," "pools of sorrows," and "waves of joys" of life transform people. As they put it, nothing is going to change the world, but meaningful words and feelings will have an impact on it, producing dreamlike images of reality. It is truly mind-boggling to contemplate that a song such as this one came from a band of young long-haired hippie musicians. Previous youth cultures, like the hippie one, have indeed had an impact on the world and cumulatively brought about a true paradigm shift across it. The song implied, moreover, that "across the universe" a new sense of meaning was emerging, leading, unconsciously, to a new universe where people of all ages are united in a common cause—a theme exploited by John Lennon in his song "Imagine." Youth culture has become a historical culture. Whether we realize it or not, we are products of the effects that the "words" and "melodies" of young people of the past have quietly had on all of us, from the flappers to the rappers.

THE DAY THE MUSIC DIED

It is relevant to return one more time to *The Catcher in the Rye*, the first insightful fictional portrait of the teenage persona. In a sanitarium, 16-year-old Holden Caulfield, a troubled, troublesome, and insubordinate adolescent who had been suspended from his preparatory school, retells the events of the few days before Christmas vacation to a psychiatrist. Disgusted by the hypocrisy of adult society, Holden's narrative penetrates the emotional essence of the rebellious adolescent mind—a mind disgusted by phoniness, insensitivity, self-indulgence, and stupidity. Holden Caulfield is an idealistic young man repulsed by the social masks that people wear and by the routine and dreary habits they constantly exhibit. His narrative ancestry can be traced to Goethe's *The Sorrows of Young Werther* (1774), Dostoyevsky's *Raw Youth* (1875), Tarkington's *Seventeen* (1916), and similar literary creations. Like these other fictional characters, Holden speaks a language uniquely his own, suffused with the voice-rhythms, turns-of-phrase, and expressions of the Romantic idealist.

All youth cultures in the twentieth century, from the flappers to the rappers, can be seen to be products of the same kind of Romantic imagination, because in one way or other they reacted in peculiar ways to the phoniness of the world. But J.D. Salinger's plea to change the hypocritical world of modern society has faded.

Before the Flapper Era, the adult world was truly adult. Its constituency had never really undergone the experience of enfolding within it a youth culture with its rebellious intent. But, as the Beatles observed, the rebellion may be over—it is difficult to rebel against rebels, since there may be nothing to rebel against.

Photo 6.2: Illustration of J.D. Salinger

Source: Time Inc., illustration by Robert Vickrey, courtesy of Wikimedia Commons

Sadly, the music may have finally died, to paraphrase again Don McLean's line in his 1971 song "American Pie." Youth culture has been a significant one, opening up the aesthetic channels to one and all, not just the elite and the cognoscenti. It made personal choice a reality. It brought about social, political, artistic, and cultural changes that would not have occurred otherwise.

Rebellion and revolution were taken literally to the streets by hippies and rappers. Rebellion in cyberspace lacks the same "grounding." Its geography is virtual and infinite, not located in a specific space or within a definite time frame. Youth cultures have always been synchronized with events and movements in politics, literature, philosophy, and the arts, as we have seen. There is no evidence that this synchronization is still functional. The pop art movement, for example, rejected in the same way the hippies did the banality that wealth and unbridled capitalism generates. It is no coincidence that the writers and the artists were young people when their works really meant something. F. Scott Fitzgerald, the Beat writers, J.D. Salinger, Andy Warhol, and the like were partners in crime with the youth rebels. New youth culture movements simply cannot be sustained in a meme culture and in a world where the mass media have lost interest in young rebels and revolutionaries, turning their attention to crimes against humanity in global conflicts, populist politics (as witnessed by the election of Donald Trump in America), unstable economies, climate change, and many more dangers that cannot be resolved simply.

Mark Bauerlein argues that the online generation is an anomaly when it comes to all previous youth generations.[15] He suggests that millennials have been born into the advantages of a prosperous technological world, loosening the hold of the past over them, and thus they may have enwrapped themselves in a generational cocoon, engaging in puerile banter rather than in any philosophical discussion of the world's issues. Similar assessments now abound.[16] On the other side, it may well be that the millennials are a more "mature" generation than any adolescents of the past.[17] Whatever the truth, change has truly occurred. The music has finally died, to extend the metaphor.

Nick Johnstone, cited several times in this book, argues that the generation that was the most radical one of all was the Rock Era. For Johnstone, it started the ball truly rolling, bringing about lasting change in a simple, yet powerful way. It did so through music. He puts it as follows:

> In short, 1956 was ground zero for pop and rock as we know it. Yes, there have been many movements in music since which nearly turned the world upside down in the same way—the hippie era, punk, grunge—but none made the world an entirely new place, in the way rock 'n' roll singers of 1956 did. That one marvelous year for music drew on everything that came before, distilled it beautifully into a new gleaming music, then fed it to a hungry global youth, who then proceeded to dance it into changing the world.[18]

The Rock Era did give teenagers their own voice in the world. The adolescents today have a new medium to express their voice—Facebook. But the message sent out in cyberspace often simply dies off with very little effect.

EPILOGUE

Cycle is the basic pattern of human history. There are many cycles in nature, from the change of seasons to the sequence of changes that a living organism passes through. The notion of cycle certainly seems to apply to any study of cultural phenomena, which seem to come and go like the seasons.

Young people have always been judged harshly by their elders. The Bible, myths, and other ancient textual sources are filled with stories about wanton or egoistic youths such as the Prodigal Son and Narcissus. Even the Greek historian Herodotus saw it necessary to include (in his *Historia*) a comment about a fretful Sumerian father who complained, in a diary, about his son's loitering and indifference towards the future. This view of the period of youth as a problematic one is the reason why previous societies have always stressed the need for young people to assume the responsibilities of adulthood at (or even before) puberty.

The emergence of youth cultures in the twentieth century may have been a reaction against this age-old attitude. This was a product of Romantic idealism—the belief that the hypocrisy of society is best exposed by young people such as a Werther and a Holden Caulfield. So what kind of idealism did the rockers of the Elvis era espouse? Rather than be overtly idealistic, they preferred to rebel, utilizing a rebel beat, a beat that can still be heard in "Blue Suede Shoes" and "Jailhouse Rock." The beat moved the teenagers, spurring them to act and think differently from their elders. Each subsequent generation developed its own rebel beat. Passing on the beat is no longer a propensity. Since the rap movement, there has been no explosive new beat in youth culture designed to shake the world to its core. Nick Johnstone, once again, articulates this state of affairs eloquently as follows:

> Maybe the world simply isn't ready for another spark yet. Maybe iTunes and the digitization of music is changing the way music is marketed, bought and listened to—even Janis Martin, the female Elvis, has a Myspace page these days. Maybe tomorrow or next year, a singer or band will come along and shake the world by its lapels, roar a new movement in music into being. Maybe even as you read this, the next

Elvis Presley, Bob Dylan, Joe Strummer, or Kurt Cobain, is sitting on a bed in a room strumming the strings of an electric guitar and singing out a cry for change and the sound of it amplified at maximum volume throughout the house, across the rooftops of neighbours, all over the same lame grey town, is a supreme thrill and in that supreme thrill, the boy smiles because he hears a way out.[19]

Youth culture has had an effect on all of us alive today. The structure of modern social systems in the countries of the Western world is a consequence of events and changes initially brought about by youths, starting in the Roaring Twenties. The blueprint for this state of affairs was designed in the 1920s. That was the era when being young and carefree gained social value—a value that has since defined the modern world.

Maybe a new and exciting youth movement with its own music is around the corner. Hopefully it will take aim at the senseless wars around the world, fruitless conflicts, and the spread of xenophobia. For now the music may have indeed died, but hopefully it is just dormant. The dream of the rock rebels was a resonating one. As Don McLean puts it in the final verse of his famous song, the time may have come to say "Bye, bye Miss American Pie."

NOTES

CHAPTER 1

1. A good overall account of the Frankfurt School is the one by Shane Gunster, "Frankfurt School and Critical Theory" in *Encyclopedia of Media and Communication*, ed. Marcel Danesi (Toronto: University of Toronto Press, 2013), pp. 289–297.

2. G. Stanley Hall, *Adolescence: Its Psychology and Its Relations to Physiology, Anthropology, Sociology, Sex, Crime and Religion* (New York: Appleton-Century-Crofts, 1904).

3. Antonio Gramsci, *Letters from Prison* (New York: Columbia University Press, 1993), p. 162.

4. Shulamith Shahar, *Childhood in the Middle Ages* (London: Routledge), p. 27.

5. Robert Epstein, *The Case Against Adolescence: Rediscovering the Adult in Every Teen* (Sanger, Ca.: Quill Driver Books, 2007), p. 3.

6. Émile Durkheim, *Suicide* (London: Routledge, 2005; originally 1897); *The Elementary Forms of Religious Life* (Paris: Presses Universitaires de France, 1912).

7. See Marcel Danesi, *Forever Young: The "Teen-Aging" of Contemporary Culture* (Toronto: University of Toronto Press, 2002).

8. Penelope Eckert, "Adolescent Social Structure and the Spread of Linguistic Change," *Language in Society* 17 (1988), p. 188.

9. Sigmund Freud, *Drei Abhandlungen zur Sexualtheorie* (Frankfurt am Main: Fischer, 1905).

10. Erik H. Erikson, *Childhood and Society* (New York: Norton, 1950); *Identity: Youth and Crisis* (New York: Norton, 1968).

11. Margaret Mead, *Coming of Age in Samoa* (New York: North American Library, 1928); *From the South Seas: Studies of Adolescence and Sex in Primitive Societies* (New York: Morrow, 1939).

12. Mead, *From the South Seas*, p. 157.

13. Robert Staughton Lynd and Helen Merrell Lynd, *Middletown: A Study in Modern American Culture* (New York: Harcourt, Brace, and World, 1929), p. 24.

14. Linda M. Scott, *Fresh Lipstick: Redressing Fashion and Feminism* (New York: Palgrave Macmillan, 2005).

15. Scott, *Fresh Lipstick*, p. 9.

16. Marshall McLuhan, *Understanding Media: The Extensions of Man* (New York: McGraw Hill, 1964).

17. See Marcel Danesi, *Brands* (London: Routledge, 2006) for a relevant discussion.

18. James B. Twitchell, *Twenty Ads that Shook the World* (New York: Crown, 2000), p. 1.

19. Herbert Marcuse, *One-Dimensional Man* (London: Routledge, 1964), p. 123.

20. Ernest Hemingway, *Death in the Afternoon* (New York: Charles Scribner's Sons, 1932).

21. F. Scott Fitzgerald, *The Crack-Up*, "Notebook E," published first in *Esquire* magazine in 1936. It was edited by Edmund Wilson after Fitzgerald's death in 1940.

22. John Morrish, *Frantic Semantics: Snapshots of Our Changing Language* (London: Macmillan, 1999).

23. Morrish, *Frantic Semantics*, p. 46.

24. Richard Huelsenbeck, "Dada Lives," in *Transition*, 25 (Autumn 1936; trans. in *The Dada Painters and Poets: An Anthology*, ed. Robert Motherwell, Bellknapp Press, 1951).

25. Greil Marcus, *Mystery Train* (New York: E.P. Dutton, 1975), p. 18.

26. André Previn, *Serious Music And All That Jazz!* (New York: Simon & Schuster, 1969), p. 12.

CHAPTER 2

1. Marcel Danesi, *Cool: The Signs and Meanings of Adolescence* (Toronto: University of Toronto Press, 1994).

2. Marcel Mauss, "Les techniques du corp," *Journal de Psychologie* 32 (1934), pp. 3–4.

3. Karl Marx, *Economic & Philosophic Manuscripts of 1844* (Moscow: Progress Publishers, 1944; originally 1844).

4. Émile Durkheim, *Suicide*.

5. Bob Dylan comment on the anniversary of Presley's death, in *US* (New York, August 1987).

6. Nick Johnstone, *A Brief History of Rock and Roll* (London: Robinson, 2007), pp. 107–108.

7. Jane Stern and Michael Stern, *Encyclopedia of Pop Culture* (New York: Harper, 1992), p. 15.

8. Thomas Doherty, *Teenagers & Teenpics* (London: Unwin Hyman, 1988), p. 46.

9. Norman Mailer, "The White Negro: Superficial Reflections on the Hipster," *Dissent*, Fall, 1957, p. 276.

10. Steven Quartz and Anette Asp, *Cool* (New York: Farrar, Straus and Giroux, 2015), p. 179.

11. Marcel Danesi, *X-Rated: The Power of Mythic Symbolism in Popular Culture* (New York: Palgrave-Macmillan, 2008).

12. Ursula K. Le Guin, "Is Gender Necessary?" in *Aurora: Beyond Equality*, ed. Susan Anderson and Vonda McIntyre (Greenwich: Fawcett, 1976), p. 24.

13. See, for example, Marcel Danesi, *My Son Is an Alien: A Portrait of Contemporary Youth* (Lanham: Rowman & Littlefield, 2003).

14. John Leland, *Hip: The History* (New York: HarperCollins, 2004).

15. Emily White, *Fast Girls: Teenage Tribes and the Myth of the Slut* (New York: Scribner, 2001), p. 24.

16. In *Cool: The Signs and Meanings of Adolescence* (Toronto: University of Toronto Press, 1994), I preferred to call the language of teens a manifestation of the "dialect" that emerges at "puberty," and hence "pubilect." An in-depth discussion of the code functions of slang can be found in Michael Adams' excellent book, *Slang: The People's Poetry* (Oxford: Oxford University Press, 2009).

17. Elizabeth Hardwick, *Bartleby in Manhattan and Other Essays* (New York: Random House, 1968), p. 48.

18. Bruce Dickinson, quoted in the *Guardian* (London, 10 Jan. 1991).

19. Johnstone, *A Brief History of Rock and Roll*, p. 70.

20. Johnstone, *A Brief History of Rock and Roll*, pp. 2–3.

21. Lawrence Grossberg, *We Gotta Get Out of This Place: Popular Conservatism and Postmodern Culture* (London: Routledge, 1992), p. 181.

22. Marty Jezer, *The Dark Ages: Life in the U.S. 1945–1960* (Cambridge, MA: South End Press, 1982), p. 23.

23. Jezer, *The Dark Ages*, p. 24.

24. J.D. Salinger, *The Catcher in the Rye* (Boston: Little, Brown, 1951), p. 19.

25. Salinger, *The Catcher in the Rye*, p. 27.

26. Jean Baudrillard, *Simulations* (New York: Semiotexte, 1983).

27. Fred Kaplan, *1959: The Year Everything Changed* (New York: Wiley, 2009); see also Dave Laing, *Buddy Holly* (Bloomington: Indiana University Press, 2009).

28. Roland Barthes, *Mythologies* (Paris: Plon, 1957).

CHAPTER 3

1. Tom Wolfe, *The Electric Kool-Aid Acid Test* (New York: Farrar, Straus, and Giroux, 1968), p. 246.

2. Max Weber, *The Protestant Ethic and the Spirit of Capitalism* (London: Unwin Hyman, 1905).

3. Carl Jung, *Analytical Psychology* (New York: Meridian, 1956).

4. John Howard, "The Flowering of the Hippie Movement," *Annals of the Academy of Political and Social Science* 382 (1969), p. 43.

5. Howard, "The Flowering," pp. 43–55.

6. Plato, *The Republic*, ed. C.M. Blackwell (New York: Charles Scribner's Sons, 1956), p. 234.

7. A good treatment of counterculture rock is the book by Sheila Whiteley, *The Space between the Notes: Rock and the Counterculture* (London: Routledge, 1992).

8. Ken Goffman, *Counterculture through the Ages: From Abraham to Acid House* (New York: Villard, 2004), p. 34.

9. Nadya Zimmerman, *Counterculture Kaleidoscope: Musical and Cultural Perspectives on Late Sixties San Francisco* (Ann Arbor: The University of Michigan Press, 2008).

10. Joseph Heath and Andrew Potter, *Nation of Rebels: Why Counter-culture Became Consumer Culture* (New York: HarperBusiness, 2005).

11. Heath and Potter, *Nation of Rebels*, p. 34.

12. Allen Ginsberg in *Time* magazine interview, 1994.

13. Gary Lachman, *Turn Off Your Mind: The Mystic Sixties and the Dark Side of the Age of Aquarius* (New York: Disinformation, 2001), p. 135.

14. Thomas Frank, *The Conquest of Cool: Business Culture, Counter-culture, and the Rise of Hip Consumerism* (Chicago: University of Chicago Press, 1997).

15. Frank, *The Conquest of Cool*.

16. Frank, *The Conquest of Cool* p. 26.

17. Marcuse, *One-Dimensional Man*, p. 18.

18. Samuel Beckett, *Endgame* (London: Grove Press, 1958), p. 20.

19. Lachman, *Turn Off Your Mind*.

20. Lachman, *Turn Off Your Mind*, pp. 396–397.

21. Lachman, *Turn Off Your Mind*.

22. Cited in Vincent Bugliosi and Curt Gentry, *Helter Skelter: The True Story of the Manson Murders* (New York: W.W. Norton and Company, 1974), p. 327.

CHAPTER 4

1. See, for example, Mikhail Bakhtin, *Speech Genres and Other Late Essays* (Austin: University of Texas Press, 1986) and *Rabelais and His World* (Bloomington: Indiana University Press, 1993).

2. Mark Gavreau Judge, *If It Ain't Got that Swing: The Rebirth of Grown-Up Culture* (New York: Spence, 2000).

3. Carl G. Jung, *Memories, Dreams, Reflections* (New York: Vintage, 1963).

4. Lachman, *Turn Off Your Mind*.

5. Ted Greenwald, *Rock & Roll: The Music, Musicians, and the Mania* (New York: Friedman, 1992), p. 45.

6. Dick Hebdige, *Subculture: The Meaning of Style* (London: Routledge, 1979).

7. Jillian Venters, *Gothic Charm School* (New York: Harper, 2009), p. 8.

8. Robin Wood, *Hollywood from Vietnam to Reagan* (New York: Columbia University Press, 1979), p. 23.

9. Paul Hodkinson, *Goth: Identity, Style and Subculture* (Oxford: Oxford University Press, 2002), p. 176.

10. See especially Bakhtin, *Rabelais and His World*.

11. Camille Paglia, *Sexual Personae* (New Haven: Yale University Press, 1990); Michel Foucault, *The History of Sexuality* (New York: Vintage, 1976–1984).

12. Madonna, quoted in *People* magazine (July 27, 1992).

13. Camille Paglia, *Sex, Art, and American Culture* (New York: Random House, 1992), p. 23.

14. Paglia, *Sex, Art, and American Culture*, p. 24.

15. See, for example, Scott, *Fresh Lipstick*.

16. bell hooks, *Black Looks: Race and Representation* (Boston: South End Press, 1992), pp. 158–159.

17. Ben Malbon, *Clubbing: Dancing, Ecstasy, and Vitality* (London: Routledge, 2001), p. 186.

18. Brian Ott and Bill Herman, "Mixed Messages: Resistance and Re-appropriation in Rave Culture," *Western Journal of Communication* 67 (2003), pp. 249–270.

19. Reto Felix, "Understanding Youth Culture: Techno Music Consumption at Live Events in Spanish Speaking Countries," *Journal of International Consumer Marketing* 16 (2004), pp. 7–38.

20. Phillip R. Kavanaugh and Tammy L. Anderson, "Solidarity and Drug Use in the Electronic Dance Music Scene," *The Sociological Quarterly* 49 (2008), pp. 181–208.

21. Ott and Herman, "Mixed Messages," p. 250.

22. Chas Critcher, "Still Raving: Social Reaction to Ecstasy," *Leisure Studies* 19 (2004), pp. 145–162.

23. Ott and Herman, "Mixed Messages," p. 256.

24. Ott and Herman, "Mixed Messages," p. 258.

25. Jacques Derrida, *Of Grammatology*, trans. G.C. Spivak (Baltimore: Johns Hopkins Press, 1976).

CHAPTER 5

1. John Leland, *Hip: The History* (New York: HarperCollins, 2004).

2. Janice Rahn, *Painting without Permission* (Westport, CT: Bergin and Garvey, 2002).

3. Rahn, *Painting without Permission*, p. 64.

4. Geneva Smitherman, *Black Talk: Words and Phrases from the Hood to the Amen Corner* (Boston: Houghton Mifflin, 2000), p. 31.

5. Marcus Reeves, *Somebody Scream* (New York: Faber and Faber, 2008), p. 13.

6. Ruth Cullen, *The Little Hiptionary* (White Plains: Peter Pauper Press, 2007), p. 54.

7. Samy Alim, "Hip-Hop Nation Language," in *Language in the USA*, ed. Edward Finegan and John Rickford (New York: Cambridge University Press, 2004), p. 389.

8. Connie Eble, "Slang," in *Language in the USA*, ed. Edward Finegan and John Rickford (New York: Cambridge University Press, 2004), p. 375.

9. Bernard Spolsky, *Sociolinguistics* (Oxford: Oxford University Press, 1998), p. 35.

10. Vivian Cook, *Accomodating Brocolli in the Cemetary: Or Why Can't Anybody Spell?* (New York: Simon & Schuster, 2005), p. viii.

11. Gwendolyn D. Pough, *Check It While I Wreck It* (Lebanon, N.H.: Northeastern University Press, 2004), p. 9.

12. Cheryl L. Keyes, *Rap Music and Street Consciousness* (Chicago: University of Illinois Press, 2004), p. 192.

13. Keyes, *Rap Music*, p. 200.

14. Reeves, *Somebody Scream*.

15. See, for example, Murray Forman and Mark A. Neal (eds.), *That's the Joint: The Hip-Hop Studies Reader* (London: Routledge, 2004).

16. Jay-Z, cited on http://www.menshealth.com/guy-wisdom/not-a-businessman-a-business-man, accessed November 29, 2016.

CHAPTER 6

1. Simon Reynolds, *Retromania: Pop Culture's Addiction to Its Own Past* (New York: Faber and Faber, 2010).

2. See Marshall McLuhan, *Understanding Media*.

3. Harold Innis, *The Bias of Communication* (Toronto: University of Toronto Press, 1968).

4. McLuhan, *Understanding Media*, p. 24.

5. Stan Cohen, *Folk Devils and Moral Panics: The Creation of Mods and Rockers* (London: MacGibbon and Kee, 1972).

6. William Gibson, *Neuromancer* (New York: Orion, 1984), p. 67.

7. Jean Baudrillard, *Simulations*.

8. Michael Benedikt, *Cyberspace: First Steps* (Cambridge, MA: MIT Press, 1991), p. 1

9. Claus J. Tully, "Growing Up in Technological Worlds: How Modern Technologies Shape the Everyday Lives of Young People," *Bulletin of Science, Technology and Society* 23 (2003), p. 445.

10. Kyongwon Yoon, "Retraditionalizing the Mobile: Young People's Sociality and Mobile Phone Use in Seoul, South Korea," *European Journal of Cultural Studies* 6 (2003), p. 329.

11. Yoon, "Retraditionalizing the Mobile," pp. 328–343.

12. In no way do I intend to put down TED Talks. I have recorded two myself. The point is that not everything can be condensed into a 15-minute talk. And the illusion that it can is a symptom of the times.

13. Barthes, *Mythologies*.

14. Limor Shifman, *Memes in Digital Culture* (Cambridge, MA: MIT Press, 2014).

15. Mark Bauerlein, *The Dumbest Generation: How the Digital Age Stupefies Young Americans and Jeopardizes Our Future* (New York: Tarcher, 2008).

16. See, for example, Chap Clark and Dee Clark, *Disconnected: Parenting Teens in a MySpace World* (Grand Rapids: Baker Books, 2007); Anastasia Goodstein, *Totally Wired* (New York: St. Martin's, 2007).

17. Don Tapscott, *Grown Up Digital* (Chicago: McGraw Hill, 2009).

18. Johnstone, *Rock and Roll*, p. 279.

19. Johnstone, *Rock and Roll*, p. 282.

INDEX